Randolph Huntington, Company J.B. Lippincott

History in Brief

Randolph Huntington, Company J.B. Lippincott

History in Brief

ISBN/EAN: 9783744733847

Printed in Europe, USA, Canada, Australia, Japan

Cover: Foto ©ninafisch / pixelio.de

More available books at **www.hansebooks.com**

HISTORY IN BRIEF

OF

"LEOPARD" AND "LINDEN,"

GENERAL GRANT'S

ARABIAN STALLIONS,

Presented to him by the Sultan of Turkey in 1879.

ALSO THEIR SONS

"GENERAL BEALE," "HEGIRA," AND "ISLAM,"

BRED BY

RANDOLPH HUNTINGTON.

ALSO REFERENCE TO THE CELEBRATED STALLION

"HENRY CLAY."

"*Stirps Arabica Vicit.*"

PRINTED FOR THE AUTHOR BY
J. B. LIPPINCOTT COMPANY.
1885.

DEDICATED TO

AND IN MEMORY OF THE LATE

GENERAL U. S. GRANT,

AND

HIS LOVE FOR HORSES.

GENERAL U. S. GRANT'S

ARABIAN STALLIONS

"LEOPARD" AND "LINDEN TREE."

ALL my life, or for fifty years, I had desired to see and examine genuine Arabian horses, such as I could know to a certainty were strictly thoroughbred Arabians. That they were rare indeed in any country I knew.

Writers upon them were very superficial, being mostly tourists or travellers, interested in geographical matters, or in the people, customs, and relics, with traditional associations, seldom if ever being horsemen, capable of judging with just comparison, if I except Sir Wilfrid S. Blunt, of England, who, as an equine investigator of remarkable ability, in company with his wife lived with the Arabs of the desert for that express purpose, and to whom I am indebted for very much valuable information upon the subject.

Different Presidents of the United States, also Secretaries of State, have at various periods received splendid horses as presents from Arabia or Turkey; the last President receiving such a gift previous to General Grant being, I believe, James K. Polk. In 1860 the late William H. Seward, while Secretary of State, had two fine specimens sent to him from Syria; but after the novelty of their arrival wore off, none could tell what had become of them, while those loudest in condemnation or ridicule of Arabian horses could neither say they had ever seen one, nor speak with personal knowledge of the get by any thoroughbred Arabian stallion. In the matter of ex-Secretary Seward's Arabians, while many were ready to condemn, few could remember having seen them; nor could any one point me to the get of either horse upon which to base credit or discredit.

Persistent inquiry, oral and by letter, after five or six years' time, gave me the first and last of Seward's two Arab horses, now dating back twenty-five years; and the information I obtained may soon startle such as are interested in "time standard" breeding rather than blood. Suffice it to say, however, that this information determined me to become personally interested in the two Arabian stallions presented to General Grant.

As General U. S. Grant outranked in the estimation of the people of the world any representative man America had produced, both as General-in-Chief of the victorious American army and as the unanimously re-elected President of our great Republic, it is but natural to suppose the Sultan of Turkey would honor himself and his Empire by presenting to the general the very choicest specimens of their idolized horses, the Arabian.

At the time of their arrival in this country I was compiling a work devoted to Old Henry Clay, to be entitled a "History of Henry Clay;" and for the purpose of having correct sketches of representative sons and daughters of the horse, had engaged Herbert S. Kittredge (since deceased), whom in 1876 I had encouraged to make horse portraiture his profession. Young Kittredge resided with me, as did later Andrew J. Schultz, who was to study under him.

When General Grant's Arabians were thoroughly recovered from their voyage and acclimated, I sent Kittredge to sketch them, as frontispieces to my "Clay History," also illustrative of blood influences; Henry Clay being but a third remove from the Arabian upon the *paternal* side, and largely *inbred* to that blood *maternally* through imported Messenger, First Consul, and Rockingham, all of which were of Godolphin Arabian blood, and Messenger himself was inbred to it.

Young Kittredge's success was wonderful. I presented copies of his sketches to General Grant, to General E. F. Beale, to Paymaster-General J. Adams Smith, and to Hon. Erastus Corning, also to one or two other gentlemen friends whom I believed trustworthy.

General Grant pronounced them "perfect to life."

General E. F. Beale wrote me:

"I return you my thanks for the pictures of Leopard and Linden. They are the best horse pictures I have ever seen, and are the most faithful likenesses, being great credit to the gifted and talented Kittredge.

"Very truly yours,
"E. F. BEALE.

"LAFAYETTE SQUARE, WASHINGTON, D. C."

As General E. F. Beale received the stallions and kept them at his place, "Ash Hill," near Washington, for three years, he was a competent critic of Kittredge's work. In a similar manner wrote Paymaster-General J. Adams Smith, of the United States Navy. General Smith being an expert horseman, and long having Grant's Arabs in charge, his opinion is of equal value. Then again, Major J. K. Levitt, for fifty years known in Philadelphia as an expert horseman and judge of horses, pronounced the two sketches by H. S. Kittredge as the most perfect likenesses of the two stallions which he had at any time seen of any horses. Mr. Levitt was the man who first received the stallions to exhibit, which he did for three months after their arrival.

I am particular in quoting these criticisms upon my sketches as exhibited in this book, because I have seen numerous prints and photographs purporting to represent General Grant's Arabian stallions, no one of which has been the least like them. My sketches are the horses to life, upon paper; and the proofs sent me by Messrs. J. B. Lippincott Company, of Philadelphia, were such excellent reproductions that I intrusted the publication of my work to them.

HOW I CAME TO ISSUE THIS BOOK.

Early in May, 1885, I received a letter from a gentleman, introducing himself as a personal friend of General Grant and his family, and, as such, requesting that I give him a transcript of my papers pertaining to the general's Arabian stallions; as to their shipment from Constantinople, date of shipment, name of vessel, commander, port of entry and date of arrival, also consignment; referring me to General Grant or either of his sons as to himself. By the next mail another letter came from the same gentleman, asking permission to publish extracts from my private letters to General Grant and his son Ulysses regarding the two stallions, and my stallions by them; also asking pictures of my young horses by Leopard and Linden.

While the refinement and courtesy of this gentleman's letter was such as to assure me of his good intent, I felt obliged to decline his request. As pirating of my expensive sketches, with plagiarism of my public writings, had been the order of the day for the past three years, I had grown recluse.

Upon reflection, and knowing the condition of General Grant, I felt that it might be some pleasure to him to see in print the information I had obtained; also the result of my experiments in breeding to his two stallions; hence I wrote two articles, which appeared during the months of May and June, 1885, in "Dunton's Spirit of the Turf," published at Chicago, and in the "California Breeder and Sportsman."

These two articles created a demand for a publication to include my sketches of General Grant's Arabians. As my Clay History would be delayed a long time for want of means to reproduce my eighty sketches representing that family, I decided to yield to the demands, and publish a book devoted to General Grant's Arabs, in so handsome a style as to become a souvenir to the memory of Grant, and encourage what he would have liked to do for the horse-breeders of America. The general was a great lover of horses, and often remarked that "he saw no reason why America should not have a national horse; but that to produce one they must go to the primitive root, the same as did England and France, also Russia,—*i.e.*, the Arabian." While his extreme modesty prevented him from suggesting that his stallions be freely used, I knew him to be very much pleased that I undertook what I did, at the time I did, and in the way I did; but the dear good man will never know what it has cost me, mentally and financially, through popular prejudice, the mighty and cruel executioner of the individual.

I will now devote my pen to the two horses Leopard and Linden Tree. The two names as I give them are the English translation of the Turkish; but in speaking of them, the word Tree is left off, making the names as given the two stallions, Leopard and Linden.

These two stallions arrived in this country May 30, 1879. They were first heard of in Philadelphia, where they were exhibited in General Grant's name.

Early in the spring of 1880 I went to Washington, D. C, to see and to examine them, also to learn if I could breed to them.

General E. F. Beale, a lifelong true and warm friend of General Grant, also a great horse-lover, had the two horses upon his beautiful farm "Ash Hill," just outside the city, and near to the Soldiers' Home.

Unfortunately, General Beale was in California, looking after his large interests upon the Pacific; but I learned that Paymaster J. Adams Smith, of the Navy Department, had the Arabs in charge, and was also a most thoroughly informed horseman. I called at the Naval Pay-Office, found the officer disengaged, and enjoyed a long and interesting conversation with him upon Arabian as well as other horses in the East, and all over the world in fact, for they seemed to have been a special study with him at every port he had visited.

It may surprise some of our so-called horse-breeders that a naval officer, who had spent most of his days at a naval academy or on board ship, should be better informed than some professional breeders upon land; but I have found it to be frequently the case with both naval and army officers. Men are born with the breeder's gift, and no matter what their calling may be, that gift is there, waiting only the opportunity for development.

Thus, Paymaster Smith was born with this gift, which had been cultivated somewhat in boyhood; then through years of observation, with comparison in the mind, at different ports of the world, he had stored away information far richer than that of men delving a lifetime in "one rut," with one idea, "upon one side of the fence."

A breeder should be a liberally-educated man, and by nature a worker, which unfortunately few are. He should be a physical worker, also a mental worker, withal a thinker: and my word for it, there is not one moment for play or recreation, scarce even for social conversation.

Some of my very best correspondents upon the questions of animal life in years gone by have been officers in the army and navy.

The question of blood and breeding in horses, cattle, sheep, and dogs is of importance to all civilized nations, which these men know; and where a naval officer is interested, his opportunities for information are rare indeed. Naval officers, as a rule, are some of our best-educated men. The system of mental training in the navy tends to make strong-minded men with retentive memories. Their restriction to confinement, I may say, in connection with study, breeds and encourages deep thought with after-reflection. Graduating from a naval academy, they visit by schooling-ships the different distant ports of the world, cultivating observation and memory. Curiosity prompts comparison, and the most important mental faculty, memory, is constantly worked. Cultivation of the three traits, observation, comparison, and memory, after the young mind and habits have been trained and cultured (refined), enhances the quality of the growing man, all being at any moment successfully applied to development of any special gift possessed, aside from the may be forced legitimate calling. Thus, the merchant, the doctor, the lawyer, or the mechanic can become a successful breeder if he has the breeder's gift; and his mental culture, with trained system, will give him a wonderful advantage over the yeoman who hates "book learning."

Paymaster (later Paymaster-General U.S.N.) Smith was by instinct a breeder and handler of horses; or, as the saying is, "was all horse" when not otherwise engaged. He was a splendid driver, and superior to most landsmen in the saddle: indeed, I considered General Beale fortunate in being able to leave General Grant's Arabians in charge of so able a gentleman, during his trip to California. Remember, this was the spring of 1880, and the horses had been at "Ash Hill" only since the fall of 1879.

I was impatient to see the Arabs; so after dinner Paymaster Smith ordered his light wagon, and as I write I think of that delightful ride to "Ash Hill." Arriving there, the smiling, happy-faced little darkies greeted us with "massa" dis and "massa" dat, as in the old days, the happiest of my life.

In front of the stables, upon a beautiful table-land overlooking acres of meadow pasturage, with scattered barns and hay-ricks, was a level spot of close, fine turf, splendid to show horses upon. Upon this the colored groom Addison led out first the Arab Leopard. He was a beautiful dapple-gray, fourteen and three-quarter hands high; his symmetry and perfectness making him appear much taller. As he stood looking loftily over the meadows below, I thought him the most beautiful horse I had ever seen. With nostrils distended and eyes full of fire, I could imagine he longed for a run upon his desert home. Addison gave him a play at the halter, showing movements no horse in the world can equal but the thoroughbred Arabian. He needed no quarter-boots, shin-boots, ankle-boots, scalping-boots, or protections of any kind; and yet the same movements this Arabian went through would have blemished every leg and joint upon an American trotting-horse, even though he had been able to attempt the to him impossible activity.

He was now brought to a stand-still that I might examine him; not cocked on one leg, pointed in another, or straddled, as our horses would be after such violent exercise, but bold and erect on all fours, as when first led out.

I began at his head. The ear was very small and fine, much as Old Henry Clay had. The muzzle was small and fine, the mouth handsome, and lips very thin, as were the nostrils. Between the eyes he was full and broad, while the eyes themselves were large, brilliant, and of the speaking kind. I lifted the lids, and they, too, were thin and delicate, not coarse and heavy, as in our big-mouthed, thick-lipped, long, heavy-eared American horse. The jowls were very deep, but wide between (so much condemned in Henry Clay). The windpipe was large and free, running low into the breast. The neck was beautifully arched, giving the impression of a thin crest, which I expected to find, from numerous writers' reports. Imagine my surprise when, upon running my hand from between the ears down, I found a big, thick, hard crest, as if a three- or even four-inch new cable-rope were inside. This was exactly such a crest as was in Old Henry Clay, which lopped over like a bag of meal with old age; and I remembered having an old Messenger stallion, years ago, with exactly such a crest, which, falling over in the same way with age, was a great torment to my pride. How I do punish myself in these days, to think of the green sheep-pelt sweats I gave this noble old Messenger stallion to get the crest so it would stay up in place! Verily, boys and young men are fools, but they do not know it.

Well, Leopard and his groom, Addison, remained perfectly still until I had run my hands over every part of the horse's body, from the tips of his ears to the bottom of his feet, even to examining the texture of his skin or hide, to see if it contained any spots. No more perfect animal ever lived than General Grant's Arabian stallion Leopard.

Now for his gaits. I had Addison lead him on the walk to and from me, say a distance of two or three hundred feet, that I might see the position of the feet in walking. There was no twisting behind, nor paddle in front, but straight, clean, elastic stepping. I now had him pass me at the side, that I might see his knee, also hock and stifle action. From the walk I had him moved upon the trot, and at either walk or trot every movement was perfect. The knee-action was beautiful: not too much, as in toe-weighted horses, nor stiff and staky, as in the English race-horse, but graceful and elastic, beautifully balanced by movement in the hock and stifle. To make Leopard a very fast trotting-horse nothing was wanting but the training from colthood, as is done with our colts of to-day. One thing we should gain by training such a colt as Leopard was, and that would be in the saving of boots with other mechanical contrivances. I could but say to myself, truly, "God has made all things perfect."

I have been accustomed to handling stallions for the past thirty years, hence look first for the disposition. At this time Leopard's disposition was excellent, or, as ladies would say, "lovely!" and "sweet!" Twice this horse has taken the first premium at the "National Horse Show of America" over his stable companion Linden.

Linden Tree (or Linden, for short) was now led out. This horse has been called a "jet-black" by some papers, which was a mistake never corrected by such journals. At that time, the spring of 1880,

Linden was a beautiful, smooth, blue-gray, which this summer of 1885 has changed to a *white*-gray.

In height he is the same as Leopard, fourteen and three-quarter hands, which is the usual height of the thoroughbred Arabian.

In build he was more compact than Leopard, being deeper and broader; of more substance, but with just as clean and fine limbs as Leopard had. The limbs, joints, and feet of both horses were perfect. The fetlocks could not be found; there were none. The warts at point of ankle were wanting, and the osselets were very small. Large, coarse osselets show cold, mongrel blood. The crest of the neck in Linden was thick and hard, the same as in Leopard. This fact will astonish some fancy horsemen, who are led to believe that a thin crest is evidence of fine breeding. My experience of late years is that a thin crest belongs to a long-bodied, flat horse, of soft constitution.

When Job said the "neck of the horse was clothed with thunder," he had reference to the Arabian horse. As the shoulder possesses the greatest strength in a horse, it is reasonable to believe the neck, to which it is joined, should have strength in harmony therewith; and this bold, stout crest of the Arab was just as God wanted it. The mane in both horses was very fine and silky, falling over so as to cause one to believe the crest was a knife-blade, with blade up, for thinness. The head of Linden was the counterpart of Leopard in all ways; as in fine, thin muzzle, lips, and nostrils; also small, fine, beautiful ears, thin eyelids; deep, wide jowls, etc.; but the face looked much older, although Linden was a year younger than Leopard.

There were two reasons for this difference in the countenance: First, the depression over the eyes in Linden was greater, which feature is said often to indicate advanced years in sire and dam when the foal was got. This would be evidence that the blood of Linden was very choice, for all breeders wish to get from their choicest-bred animals as long as is possible, even to extreme old age; and some of the finest horses I have ever seen have been produced by dams thirty-six and one thirty-eight years old. If I did not know these to be facts I would not repeat them in this book.

To intensify the effect of depression over the eyes in Linden were large black markings or rings around them, which at a little distance made him look at this time very old; with me, from what I now knew of Arabian horses, these marks intensified his blood value. I quote from Sir Wilfrid S Blunt, in Lady Anne Blunt's beautiful work entitled "The Bedouin Tribes of the Euphrates": "These black markings are

held by the Arabs of the desert as evidence that the animal is of the thoroughbred Bint El Ahwaj breed, descending from the children of Ishmael, and from which breed came the Godolphin Arabian, and which Godolphin Arabian was in part founder of the French Percheron horse, also of the best strains of the English thoroughbred running-horse; and to which Godolphin Arabian imported Messenger was three times close bred, and very close at that in both sire and dam. Of course Arabian statements are traditionary, but facts in that country go strongly to support their traditions. This breed of which I am speaking, identified by the black markings around the eyes, are also known as the Kehilans, from these markings having the appearance of being painted with kohl, after the fashion of the Arab women; hence the desert name of Kehilans.

"The name of Kochlani is credited to King Solomon's stud; but they have a breed in Persia by this name, which, although they are Arabian horses, are impure."

From all I have been able to learn from abroad, it is most likely that the two horses represent the two thoroughbred breeds of "Kehilan" and "Kochlani," the two choicest of the desert.

I have tried to impress the reader with the feeling that I considered Linden the better horse of the two, and will give my reasons.

During the inspection of the Sultan's choicest horses, General Grant, who had an excellent eye, with judgment, expressed great admiration for the beautiful colt Leopard, and it was presented to him by the Sultan. Of course General Grant did not understand the Turkish or Arabic language, and could not comprehend any breeding given to him. His choice or selection had been entirely governed by superior beauty with wonderful perfection in the colt. After having presented Leopard to the general, the Sultan desired to make a special present of his own selection; and holding General Grant in the highest possible esteem as General-in-Chief of the victorious United States army under him, and also knowing him to have been twice President of this great American people, the Sultan would naturally have an individual as well as a national pride that his special present should be the best possible specimen of blood and breeding to be had through his power; and he knew what General Grant could not understand, that Linden represented blood which time would prove of more excellence than in Leopard. Under the circumstances, does any man suppose the Sultan would insult himself and his power by presenting an inferior selection to General Grant's necessarily ignorant choice? Every breeder can understand this argument from selections made by gentlemen fanciers from stock he has bred and raised. It is pretty hard work to tell a gentleman who at first sight "knows it all" that he knows very little; but General Grant was not of that class, to assume knowledge. Since arrival in this country, the superior beauty and grace of Leopard has had a tendency to dwarf Linden in public opinion, encouraged through the influence of printer's ink. He has been credited with being vicious, which the newspapers were very noisy about at one time, in and over a suit brought against General Grant for keeping such a horse.

During the early spring and summer of 1880, also in 1881, I handled the two stallions many times in and out of their boxes at "Ash Hill," at which time I had my mares there to breed, but never at any moment considered Linden vicious. I knew that he was all horse, and that as a stallion his disposition needed watching and nursing with a kind but firm hand. Petulant words, with habitual scolding, makes many a stallion ugly; and many a groom is more at fault than the brute. Arabian stallions are very sensitive to words, quickly appreciating the kind, cheerful good-morning. The human voice has a wonderful influence over the brute, and cross, ugly words they will in time resent.

As I have remarked, I put these two stallions through their gaits many times, finding Linden the best at walk or at trot, because more even and steady.

At the "National Horse Show" in New York City, I have said Leopard was twice awarded a first premium over Linden, to which by individual comparison he was entitled.

The judge who would pronounce otherwise before four or five thousand people would be called very incompetent: but looks are deceptive.

I bred six mares to these two Arabian stallions in 1880 and 1881, getting three horse colts and one filly. I selected kindred blood as found in Old Henry Clay's daughters and inbred granddaughters. I handled the foals from the time they were born. Three were by Linden and one by Leopard. Not one of them is ugly or inclined to be vicious. All are broken, and not one has at any time offered to kick or to strike, although the dams of each one were high-strung, high-tempered mares, two of them particularly so. I found these Arab colts, while very small, required different treatment from mongrels, hence haltered and handled them myself up to this present time, in and about the stable, for that is the place the disposition is improved or spoiled. When two years old, my daughter could drive the son of Leopard anywhere, for he was fearless and reliable.

I will now speak particularly of the colors of Arabian horses. I have before said that one of General Grant's stallions had been reported through a leading daily paper as "*jet-black*." Hundreds who read that, will believe it and report it for fifty years to come, until it becomes traditional. It is a bad mistake, as a black Arabian is an unusual color, and denotes inferiority. I will quote again from Sir W. S. Blunt: "Bay with black points, and with generally a white foot, or two or three white feet, and a snip or blaze down the face, are prominent among the Anazeh or Bint El Ahwaj breed. Grays are also common, then chestnut of different shades. The spotted, or piebald, or parti-colored horses are unknown among the pure Arabs. The pure white is very highly prized."

At birth, the gray horse is black; and the true black horse is born of a brown shade. In the first moulting, the proper color shows itself to the breeder. The dapple-gray will show gray at the first moulting, but the blue-gray and black-gray will carry a black coat into the second and third moulting, the black hairs always shedding first, so that the novice is frequently puzzled to tell what colored horse he is to have at maturity. The blue-gray grows to a white gray, but the dapple-gray holds its distinctive color longest, as a rule.

Having bred my mares to General Grant's Arabs in the spring of 1880, I became quite anxious to know all particulars relating to them, lest in future days some as yet unborn writer should tell his readers that General Grant's horses were genuine imported Barbs, or maybe Andalusian horses, when any old man knowing to the contrary would be disputed into silence. The pedigrees of our horses credit Arabian blood frequently in some of the fastest and most valued animals; but attempt to unravel such breedings, and one lands among the "said to be's," which is not the case in England, or in Russia, or in France. They breed thoroughbreds of various kinds, and tell you how they are bred to a certainty; while with us, the time standard for the present generation settles it all, in which blood is of no value except in the black article known as printers' ink.

In fifteen years after Seward's Arabs were imported, any authentic information as to their blood and breeding, their whereabouts, or their get, was a difficult matter to get at. The same was the case with those of James K. Polk, and so it has been in many instances where I have investigated. If Arabian blood was of value to England, to France, and to Russia, so it could be to America, for certainly we have not the self-sustaining types in horses to do credit to any civilized country as have the nations cited. Should we export our present horses?

Having obtained all I could from Paymaster Smith, I awaited General E. F. Beale's return from California. From him I did not get what I wanted. I then wrote to General Grant himself, and give below his reply.

"LONG BRANCH, N. J., July 28, 1882.
"RANDOLPH HUNTINGTON, Rochester, N. Y.

"DEAR SIR,—About my Arabian horses, I cannot answer all your questions, but what I know I will give you.

"I was in Constantinople in March, 1878, and visited the Sultan, and with him his stables.

"All of his horses were of the most approved and purest blood (and there were about seventy horses in the stables I visited). I was told that the pedigrees of all of them ran back from five to seven hundred years (in breed).

"Two of the horses that I then saw were sent to me as a present from the Sultan by the first steamer directly to the United States from that port. I do not know the name of the steamer, nor the date of its departure or arrival. They (the horses) were consigned to General E. F. Beale, of Washington City, who can probably inform you upon those points. Leopard was five years old when I first saw him, and Linden four, I think. I am certain as to the age of the first, and think I am right about the age of the second.

"The fact of these horses being from the Sultan's own private stables, and being a present from him as an appreciation of our country among the nations of the earth, is the best proof of the purity of their blood.

"Very truly yours,
"U. S. GRANT."

I now knew that neither General Grant, General Beale, nor Paymaster-General Smith could give me the identifying facts I wanted for fifty years hence.

I remembered hearing my cousin, Mrs. Dr. Anderson, of New Haven, Connecticut, say to me one day while visiting there, that General Grant had two horses arrive at that port by a foreign vessel, and that they were said to be Arabians. Upon which she went to the doctor's desk and took out some nails his blacksmiths had given him when they removed the shoes to re-shoe the stallions.

As these remarks were incidental with other subjects at the time, I paid no special attention to them; but memory often comes to our help, so I addressed a letter to William D. Anderson, M.D., New Haven, Connecticut, and below give his reply:

"RANDOLPH HUNTINGTON, Rochester, N. Y.

"DEAR SIR,—I would say in reply that the Arabian stallions for General Grant were shod by my blacksmiths, Messrs. Palmer & Bishop, in this city of New Haven, Connecticut, on May 31, 1879; that they (the horses) having arrived the day before direct from Constantinople by the steamer Norman Monarch, Dunscomb, commander. The steamer at that time was chartered to freight cartridges, guns, etc., to Turkey, from the Winchester Arms Company in this city.

"She (the Norman Monarch) made the trip direct, entering and clearing at this port. My blacksmith went on board and removed the shoes from the horses, then took the stallions to his shop, where they were re-shod and kept in his stables until delivered to Mr. J. K. Levitt, of the Blue Bell, Darby Road, Philadelphia, Pa., and from where he exhibited them until delivered to General E. F. Beale at Washington City, for account of General U. S. Grant.

"Truly yours,
"WILLIAM D. ANDERSON, M.D.

"NEW HAVEN, CONN., August, 1882."

I next called upon Major J. K. Levitt, of Philadelphia, who told me that in June, 1879, while driving a race at the Belmont Park, Mr. Edwards called upon him with a despatch from General Beale, requesting that he should go with Mr. Edwards to New Haven for two horses for General Grant. That they brought them by boat to New York, and thence to Philadelphia. That they were shown two weeks at Suffolk Park, then at their fair, which association paid him for the exhibit. Next the fair at Dover, Delaware, gave him two hundred dollars and expenses to exhibit there. He then exhibited them a week at the Washington, D. C., Agricultural Fair; then at the fair at Alexandria, Virginia. Next at the fair at Cumberland, West Virginia, and lastly at the Doylestown Fair of Pennsylvania.

It now being late in the fall of 1879, Major Levitt ceased to care for the horses, delivering them into the possession of General E. F. Beale at Washington, D. C., to remain.

I have been particular in following up these two Arabian stallions presented to General Grant. I deemed their blood of important value to us. I would not condemn such breeders as ridicule Arabians, but would ask questions.

If Arabian blood is of no value, why does England go back in her records to so many importations of Arabian horses to create and sustain her national thoroughbred running-horse? Why does Russia take pride in referring to her Orloff trotting-horse as of Arabian origin? Why does France, through government statistics, show that her famous Percheron draught-horse is moulded from the pliable blood of the Arabian?

When men condemn Arabian horses, let them cease to extol Messenger, Diomed, Duroc, American Eclipse, Sir Archy, Boston, or Lexington, each of which owed its greatness to Arabian blood; Diomed and Messenger being, as the reader knows, close-bred to the Arabian, and Messenger, which name has been the mouth-piece for our breeders and horsemen for seventy-five years, was three times inbred to the Godolphin Arabian.

Young men think there has been wonderful improvement in our horses during the past thirty years. I do not think so. When I take up the little horse-shoe nail, but a trifle heavier than an old-fashioned shawl-pin, or examine the shoe, the harness, the sulky, the tracks, the system of training, with other improved advantages towards increased rates of trotting speed, and then look at our inferior coach-horses, and know the difficulty in obtaining even an ordinarily good pair, I must say that our horses have degenerated, while our mechanical ingenuity towards increased speed has augmented. That the number of trotting-horses is greater than a few years ago, is because we have a greater number of horses; and because one hundred are now trained for speed where one was twenty years ago.

England, Scotland, France, and Russia have each a typical horse, capable of reproducing its type with excellence in any land to which it may be exported. They are the thoroughbred race-horse, the Clyde, and the Percheron draught-horses, and the Orloff trotting-horse. Every one of these types is a thoroughbred in its country, based upon the Arabian; and, exported to any land, will reproduce itself physically and instinctively, which our time-standard bred horses will not do at present.

What we would term our national horse is of no positive blood, or instinctive value. It cannot and will not reproduce itself in a creditable manner to export as our national horse. Our system of breeding is one of great mongrelization, which, as I have repeatedly written, means uncertainty with degeneracy.

Our vast territory demands more horses than any other country. Our unlimited grass lands invite and encourage the breeding of horses, whether the owner of the lands be adapted as a breeder or not. Our varied climates and soil, with everywhere abundant and excellent water, are most favorable to the raising of all kinds of stock for export.

The producing of *specialties* in the horse is demanded by our uses, as well as required for general purposes.

The demand for coach-horses increases as our city people multiply and wealth increases. A high form of coach-horse is in constant demand, but exceedingly difficult to find. Such a horse is always a first-class farm-horse, and can be a first-class road-horse, profitable to every farmer to breed and to raise.

Our territory is so great, and our commercial interests so scattered and extended, that the road-horse becomes an important feature, so connected with commercial and agricultural pursuits that it should be cultivated. Our great national sport is the trotting-race, which in England is the running-race. The race- or running-horse is good for the one purpose of running races. The trotting-horse can be used for every purpose except running races; hence to me it seems proper it should become our national horse, to come under the intelligent head of blood and breeding with instinctive trot.

A positive thoroughbred trotting-bred horse is a possibility; and the independent nature of the American people is such I feel they should take a national pride in creating a national horse, independent of any other nation. The Arabian horse, as we know, is the foundation upon which England established her race-horse, Russia her trotting-horse, and France her draught-horse.

We have proven that from the Arabian we can get the highest rates of trotting speed. We know that its blood and instinct are more pliable to man's demands, for moulding into different families, than are either of the European types cited. We know that our so-called trotting-horse is not a positive reproducer of that ability. We know that each exceptional case of high trotting speed traces to the Arab not far away; we know that the reunion, or bringing together of bloods akin, of close affinity, gives the strongest results.

Thus, when the blood of Henry Clay (which was but a third remove from the Arab) is bred to itself, increased speed is a certain result, and when reinforced with fresh Arabian blood, a higher type is the result, with the trotting instinct intensified.

The law in animal life as relates to breeding of positive types is once away from a primitive blood, then three times back to it through different channels.

As I have said, the horse Henry Clay was but a third remove from an imported Arabian, *paternal*, and more than thrice back upon the *maternal* side. If his dam, Lady Surry, be discounted by some, they must remember she was far above the old "Vintner mare" which has figured so disparagingly in the English race-horse maternal foundation.

Through Henry Clay's daughters, granddaughters, and great-granddaughters we enlist the immortal names of Andrew Jackson and Henry Clay in dams. As the male since the first of man has given the name and founded the family, what more appropriate start could be made for a laudable and positively independent national horse than by bringing the foundation blood in the Andrew Jackson, Henry Clay daughters, to a union with the pure, primitive, unquestioned blood of General Grant's Arabian stallions?

By so doing we should honor ourselves in our to be national horse, through three of the greatest names our country has possessed.

First comes that of General U. S. Grant, known and respected by all the nations of the earth, also loved by over fifty millions of people as no other great captain ever was. On the maternal side we have the General and ex-President in Jackson, who knew no fear; and in Henry Clay a statesman without a peer. It is a singular coincidence that we should have these three immortal, national names attached to representative horses direct from the primitive horse, and independent of any other nation, from which and upon which to found and create "The National Thoroughbred Trotting-bred horse of America!" General Grant, Andrew Jackson, and Henry Clay.

The following transcript from English records, relating to the founding and establishing of their thoroughbred running-horse, may be interesting to many; so I take the liberty of copying it from the London "Field" of some time since. It will be noticed that from the early attempts in England to establish a thoroughbred running-horse they had great difficulty, owing to internal and external wars, with many troubles recorded in history; but that they depended entirely upon Arabian blood the following transcript will show. The same was the case in Russia for the creating of their thoroughbred Orloff trotting-horse, which records are very interesting and more authentic than are the early English records. So, too, in France, in matter of their Percheron, they are more definite. In Russia and in France the government gave support to the attempts, once the individuals had laid the foundation; but in each case the plastic Arabian blood had to be resorted to.

ARAB HORSES AND THE TURF.

"SIR,—I am unable to say precisely when the Royal Stud at Tutbury fell into the hands of the Parliamentarians; but it must have been some time prior to July, 1643, as on the 23d of that month four Government commissioners, viz., Mildemay, Lemprière, Carteret, and Grafton, arrived at the stud for the purpose of making a true inventory of the race-horses kept there, 'being part of the late king's personal estate.' Four days after the date of their arrival the inventory was completed, and was duly signed and sealed by each of those inquisitors. Apparently the work was done in a slovenly and careless manner, and it is probable serious mistakes were occasionally committed by the commissioners in confusing the names of the stallions with those of the animals enumerated in the catalogue, and *vice versâ*. This inventory, or catalogue, though most interesting, is too long to transcribe here in detail; suffice it to say that it consisted of one hundred lots, comprising twenty-three mares and their foals, fifteen mares four years old and upwards, sixteen three-year-old fillies and colts, seventeen two-year-old fillies and colts, twenty-two yearling fillies and colts, and twenty-three horses four years old and upwards: one hundred and thirty-nine head, all told. No specific mention of any stallion occurs in the inventory (except, as in some cases it may be inferred, that the name of the stallion, and not that of the *lot*, was intended to be given), hence it is probable that the sires were removed and kept at some other place at the time this inventory was taken. A valuation of each lot is given,—the whole amounting to nineteen hundred and eighty-two pounds, or an average of not quite fourteen guineas per head.

"There is no doubt whatever that many of those lots were immediately descended from the Digby and Villiers Arabs previously referred to, of which the latter had been imported by James I., towards the latter end of his reign. Let us take a few instances: (Lot 5) 'Black Morocco. One black mare with a few white haires in the forehead, 5 yeares old, with a horse foale, £22.' (Lot 9) 'Morocco. One brown bay mare with a starre, two white heels behind, 12 yeares old, with a horse foale, £25.' (Lot 24) 'Young Morocco. One bay mare without white, 4 yeares old, with a horse foale, £16.' (Lot 35) 'Black Morocco. One black mare without white, 10 yeares old, £10.' (Lot 52) 'Morocco. One browne bay horse with a little starr, 5 yeares old, £30.' Here we see the same name given to lot 9 and lot 52, the former a twelve-year-old mare, the latter a five-year-old horse, by which it is evident that the stallion, and not the name of the lot in the inventory (as in a modern Tattersall catalogue), was intended to be given. 'Browne Newcastle' likewise precedes lot 6 and lot 22, the former a 'browne bay mare without white, 6 yeares old, with a mare foale, £15;' and the latter a 'browne bay mare without white, 7 yeares old, with a mare foale, £23.' The highest valuations in the catalogue were put upon the produce of Rupert, an Arab stallion belonging to the Villiers 'race,' lots 53, 64, 66, and 69 in rotation, which are described as follows: 'One bright bay horse, with a starr and a snip, 4 white feete, black list downe the back, 4 yeares old, £35. One browne bay [horse] without white, 4 yeares old, £35. One browne bay horse, 4 yeares old, with a starre, £25. One bright bay horse with a black list, and one white foote, £25.' It is evident some of Sir John Fenwick's famous Arabian 'race' were introduced into the royal racing stud, as I find lot 25 is entered thus: 'Sorrell Fennick [so spelt by the Duke of Newcastle in his Magnum Opus], one Sorrel mare with a blaze, 9 yeares old, with a mare foale, £18.' So also with the celebrated Arab stud maintained at this time, and subsequently after the Restoration, at Welbeck Abbey by the Duke of Newcastle, as indicated by lots 2, 3, 6, 18, 22, 26, 59, 61, 96, 98, and 99, from which we may infer (taken with other corroboratory evidence) that the royal mares in King Charles's stud were occasionally served by stallions belonging to those notable breeders in the seventeenth century. Upon the whole, this inventory, though imperfectly and carelessly drawn up, proves that the principal, and probably the subordinate lots at the royal stud, immediately prior to the year 1643, were derived from and represented in the Arab blood, which was deemed *indispensable* by the best breeders of those days. As to the yearlings, the two-year-old and the three-year-old colts and fillies, from lot 36 to lot 49, no reference is made to either sire or dam, the color, marks, age, and valuation of each lot only being recorded. But lots 68 and 72—the former a three-year-old gray colt, valued at twelve pounds, the latter a three-year-old bay colt, valued at fifteen pounds—were got by Frisell, a son of the Markham Arabian. (Frisell is also mentioned as the stallion of lot 14—'a bright bay mare, with a streake, 12 yeares old, with a horse foale, £22.') The other yearlings, two- and three-year-old colts and fillies, from lot 73 to lot 95, are simply described and valued, without any clue of their names or parentage being given. It is unfortunate that these omissions should have occurred, particularly as the sequestrators, by a little trouble and inquiry, could have obtained the necessary information from Mr. Gregory Julian, who, as yeoman of the stud, was still in office, although the Marquis of Hamilton, and many of the officials previously mentioned, had ceased to exercise their several duties at erst royal haras. It may be, however, that the omissions to which I have referred as occurring in the two contemporary transcripts of this inventory which I have had access to—one in the Record Office, the other in the Victoria Tower, House of Lords—are supplied in the original document preserved among the Marquis of Salisbury's manuscripts at Hatfield, which I have not seen.

"Such was the state of the king's stud at Tutbury when the inventory was finished, July 27, 1649. Prior to this date, however, a bay horse, three years old, and a black horse, five years old, by Newcastle, had been 'taken up' by Quartermaster Tomlinson. These were returned to the stud, and figure in the inventory at a valuation of thirty pounds each. Colonel Sanders obtained two black horses, five years old, and a bay mare 'with a tanned mussell, 8 years old, with a mare foale,' which remained in his custody, the horses being valued at twenty pounds each, and the mare and foal at sixteen pounds.

"No time was lost by the authorities in London in taking action as to the future of the ex-royal stud. On July 31 the Council of State at Whitehall had the inventory under consideration, when it was decided that in consequence of the great destruction of horses during the late wars, and as Tutbury was 'the only place in England' where provision could be made of a good breed, and the sale of the stock at this time preserved there would not equal what it amounted to in the way it was then used, the Council determined not to sell off the horses until further consideration. This decision was received with general satisfaction, for the Roundheads liked a good horse as much as the Cavaliers. And it may be noted that in suppressing horse-racing, the Parliamentarians were not actuated by any innate antipathy to the Turf, as they were constrained to do so chiefly owing to the excuse which a projected race meeting presented to the Royalists to assemble, under cover of the sport, to disseminate sedition. Indeed, they but followed the example of the Royalists in that respect, for it is on record that General Sir Jacob Astley suppressed a race meeting at Berwick in the spring of 1639, which was projected by the Scotch Covenanters chiefly as a rendezvous to mass their forces in a favorable position to resist the king's army.

"Turning from this digression to the vicissitudes of the royal stud at Tutbury in 1649, the next thing we hear of it was when the House of

Commons, on August 29, passed a vote of thanks to Colonel Jones on the occasion of his recent victory over the forces of the Duke of Ormond in Ireland, coupled with a pension of one thousand pounds a year to him 'and his heyres for ever in Ireland;' and 'six of the best horses in Titbury race to be selected and sent to him, as a gratuity from the House.' This draft was duly selected and sent to Ireland, and it is a singular fact that some years afterwards, five of these half-dozen royal stud barbs were acquired by the Earl of Thomond, by whom the strain was carefully preserved, which doubtless accounts for the many victories won by the race-horses owned and bred by the O'Briens in England and Ireland after the Restoration, and on to the beginning of the present century. Throughout the autumn of 1649 and the spring of 1650, much solicitude was evinced by the Council of State in the welfare of the Tutbury establishment, upon the choice treasures contained wherein Oliver Cromwell was casting covetous eyes. Many other lords and commoners followed the Protector's lead in that respect; so much so, that the Council were induced to appoint a committee to consider how the stud 'may be so disposed that the breed be not lost.' This committee consisted of the Earl of Salisbury, Lords Howard, Lisle, and Grey, Sir Arthur Haselrigge, Sir William Constable, Sir William Armyne, Sir H. Mildmay, Colonel Morley, Mr. Bond, and Mr. Scott. They appear to have done nothing except to dismiss Gregory Julian, and in his stead to appoint Major Edward Downes, to whom the whole business of the stud was committed. But the final dispersal now approached apace, as on the 2d of July Cromwell obtained six of the best horses, and on the following day, a draft from the colts were 'chosen' for him. It is unnecessary here to follow all the incidents of the dispersal, as it will be sufficient to mention that on December 9, Downes, the custodian, received final instructions to dispose of the remaining animals at the best prices obtainable; but he was to allow Lord Grey 'to be furnished' with whatever lots he desired without prejudice to the sale. By January 5, 1651, all the animals were sold and distributed; the money derived by the sale was handed over to the Council of State. Downes was paid off and dismissed, when the royal stud at Tutbury, founded by James I., and so well sustained by his successor, ceased to exist. It is a remarkable circumstance that in many instances those who obtained drafts from the Tutbury stud, and bred from the strain, were conspicuous in offering to contribute, in kind, towards the resuscitation of the royal stud, nine years later on, when the king 'enjoyed his own again.' At this time the Tutbury strain was distributed over many parts of the country, and although there was no public racing, unremitting attention was paid by those possessing 'royal mares' and 'Tutbury stallions' to preserve the breed pure and undefiled. But the most remarkable, and by far the most important, contribution to Charles II.'s racing stud was the magnificent animal above mentioned, which Oliver Cromwell had obtained from Tutbury in July, 1650. During this interval of the Lord Protector's sway, he was one of the greatest breeders of thoroughbred stock, first at Hampton Court, and afterwards at New Hall in Essex. In this interval Cromwell imported many Arabian stallions. His White Turk was one of the most celebrated sires of the Commonwealth. Cromwell's weakness for Arab horses was well known to Mazarin, so much so, that on one occasion, when the crafty cardinal wanted to circumvent Colonel Lockhart (the ambassador of England at the French court), he overcame the envoy's diplomatic scruples by presenting him 'with four exceedingly fine Arab horses for the saddle,' which his Excellency pronounced to be the finest he ever saw, adding that 'his lord and master would be mightly pleased with them.' Thus we find in Cromwell's stud not only the choice animals of Tutbury,— the royal mares, horses, and colts, and their descendants which have been carefully bred therein during those nine years,—but frequent additions of new Arab blood, from which the highest breeding advantages were expected, and doubtless attained. At any rate, the fame of Cromwell's stud was well known to the merry monarch, as almost the first order he issued at the Restoration was that those horses, 'said to be the best in England,' should be seized, and returned to the royal stud. The result of that order is well known, and all horses, except Coffin Mare, soon after became the personal property of Charles II., and formed the nucleus of his racing establishment, which subsequently turned out so many winners on the race-courses of his kingdom during his remarkable reign.

"J. P. H."

GENERAL GRANT'S ARABIAN STALLIONS.

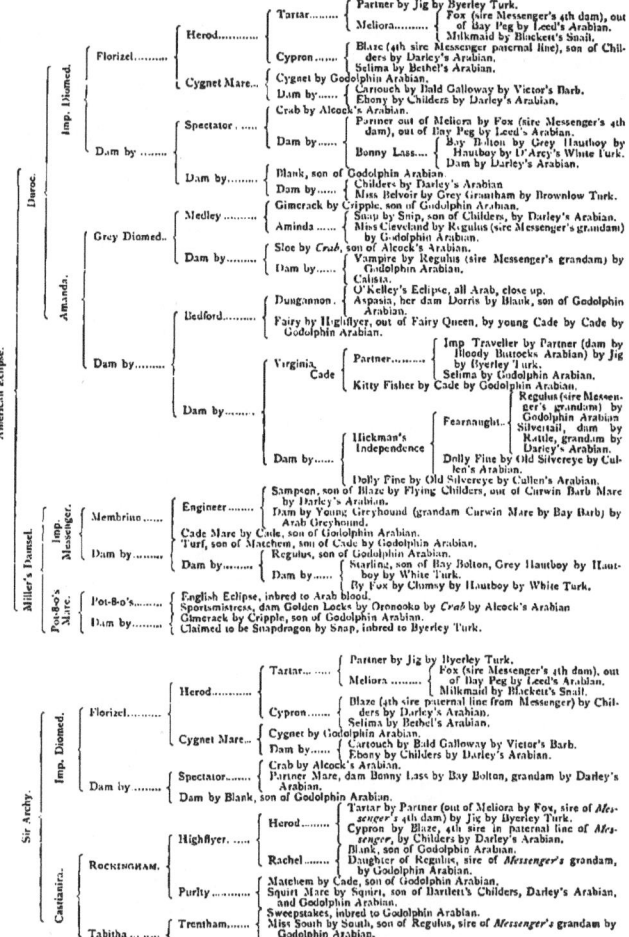

"GENERAL BEALE," "HEGIRA," AND "ISLAM,

STALLION SONS OF GENERAL U. S. GRANT'S ARABIANS "LEOPARD" AND "LINDEN,"

AND THEIR DAUGHTER

"C L A Y R A B I A,"

ALSO GRANDDAUGHTER

"C L A Y B E A L E   G R A N T."

BEALE is a golden sorrel, marked with a handsome straight white stripe in the face, gray at the root of the tail, a long white dash under the brisket, two white ankles forward, and nigh hind white sock. He was foaled June 25, 1881; was got by Leopard from Mary Sheppard, a black-roan mare fifteen and one-quarter hands high, by Jack Sheppard by Henry Clay, from his own daughter. Beale is fifteen hands high.

Hegira is a coal-black, with faint star and white on all four feet. He was got by Linden from Nell Pixley by Henry Clay; was foaled July 9, 1882, and stands fifteen and one-quarter hands high at three years old. Nell Pixley, his dam, was bred by Supervisor Pixley, of Monroe County, New York. She is fifteen and one-half hands high, strong.

Islam is a dark chestnut, with two white ankles behind. He was got by Linden from Nell Andrews by Red Bird by Henry Clay; was foaled May 12, 1882, and stands fifteen hands high at three years old. His dam is also a dark chestnut, with two white ankles behind and stripe in the face; and her dam was also a dark chestnut mare inbred to Morgan blood. The dam of Islam is fifteen and one-quarter hands high.

Clayrabia is an iron-gray without white. She was by Linden from Mag Wadsworth by Colonel Wadsworth by Henry Clay, from Colonel's own daughter. Clayrabia is fifteen hands and her dam fourteen and one-half hands high. Clayrabia was foaled July 14, 1881, and is much larger than her dam.

Claybeale Grant is a chestnut, with stripe in the face and three white legs, the nigh one forward and two behind. She was by General Beale, already mentioned and described: she is also his first get. The dam of Claybeale Grant is Nell Andrews, who was also the dam of Islam by Linden, and Islam was her virgin foal. Claybeale is the last of three foals from Nell, and is the largest at same age of the three; and while all three were perfect and beautiful, this daughter of General Beale is the handsomest foal I have ever seen, except General Beale by Leopard, from Mary Sheppard.

It has been a challenging question to me since the spring of 1880, why I bred to General Grant's Arabians?

Now having told the reader what I got, and a little of the dams, I will try to explain my reasons; also what governed me in the selection of dams for the purpose. It was by no means an impulsive move upon my part, but the result of long-considered, intelligent reasoning.

Had I anticipated the abusive condemnation I was to draw upon myself, and the privations to be suffered, resulting even in financial embarrassment in the end, through a necessary holding of the stock for the purpose of just estimation of individual values before reproduction,—in fact, a thorough knowledge of the blood instinct, with constitutional fitness for reproduction in each individual case,—added to which was to be incessant physical and mental application, without one single day of rest, with now and then sporting-paper attacks upon an exceedingly sensitive nature, I hardly think my courage would have been equal to the undertaking; nor would it have been except through faith.

God has so ordered things that it is not always men of large means who accomplish great results through discoveries, rediscoveries, or inventions; nor are improvements in already adapted and adopted discoveries and inventions made by such men; but their wealth does become the means through which they become recognized.

Since the days of King Solomon there is no record of men of wealth having become direct instruments in important scientific or mechanical progress, because they could see no immediate money returns. There are, however, occasional instances of men of grand latent natures, with noble impulses, who, having concentrated their energies upon the getting of wealth, and finding in their latter days that "all this was but vanity and vexation of spirit," and realizing their deficiencies as men, have tried to, in a measure, atone for previous neglects through legacies of large sums of money or property from their accumulations to educational or charitable institutions. Now, the simple commission upon distribution of such donations would, if given during their lifetime, have conduced greatly to their pleasure and credit, even to insuring the completion of some great enterprise which had failed for want of means at the very moment when prompt, liberal assistance would have caused a triumphant success, benefiting their country.

Courage was planted in man's nature to enable him to accomplish. It is essential to success; but with courage must be enthusiasm, which latter is to courage what fire is to water for steam,—the direct motive-power.

My main reason for breeding to General Grant's Arabs was the hope that something should grow into a national value from the Arabian blood. To give other reasons in detail necessarily involves reflections covering a lifetime, hence my writings will be tiresome to uninterested persons.

My prominence through sporting journals for many years has caused some to call me visionary; these men, however, were hardly students of animal life, but were intent listeners at the battery which clicked the changes in the money or stock values, in which their life was absorbed. This class have called me enthusiastic, forgetting that but for their own enthusiasm with concentrated thought they would not be so devoted to the one idea of money-getting, to the sacrifice of all else, even to their better natures.

My worst enemy has been the public executioner, prejudice, who can have no reason why he should or should not kill, but to kill!

The people ask, Why did you breed to General Grant's Arabs?

Permit me to say, first of all, that I am a firm believer in Bible history, as the oldest authentic records known to man. This history dates in Arabia, where all created life was first named; and here the horse known to man has been called, for all time, the Arabian horse, and, as such, the one uniformly perfect horse. All things by God were made perfect. Nothing made by Him had to be made over. Of all types of horses, the Arabian is the only one so plastic and mollient in its nature, mental and physical, as to be successfully used by man for the producing of varieties. No other type of horse can be moulded so quickly into other self-sustaining ones. Attempts with other of *man's* created forms can produce sub-varieties, only as the one same plastic affinity blood of the Arabian be intensified in the product, through union in the parents: but this requires greater time, with more uncertain results; and one may well exclaim, "Life is too short for the experiment." Moreover, through such subdivision attempts by man new disorders, mental and physical, are caused, through a violation of Nature's (God's) laws. Our greatest results are through a close relation to the ever self-sustaining, primitive blood, or positive God-power in an original type.

Let me cite different types of horses as we may know them to be a result of man's work; keeping in mind as we write or read that the executioner, prejudice, stands always ready to dispute what it cannot understand, and to kill!

Now, refer to the transcript introduced a few pages back, from the largest paper of the kind in the world, the London "Farm, Field, and Garden." That transcript is of authentic records, and by them we know the English thoroughbred race-horse was a direct product from Arabian blood, through repeated resort to it; and that the English thoroughbred race-horse was not indigenous to that country, which very many otherwise intelligent men in this country devoted to race-horses make superficial horse-fanciers and breeders believe.

Now again, this English race-horse was produced to run races, and for no other purpose. His mental and physical whole was rigidly moulded by man, from the Arabian, into what he is to-day; and to retain these qualities to their highest excellence, he is by law inbred to his own blood.

When at last he had become a self-sustaining type, he was named "the English thoroughbred race-horse," and recognized as their "national horse," devoted exclusively to their national sport of running races; and as chance, or gambling, is one of the prominent instincts of man, this horse became exclusively a gambling horse; hence the national sporting laws demanded that he be consecutively inbred to his own blood. *But one* blood could be introduced as legitimate and proper, and that was of God's horse,—*the Arabian*, or primitive.

When this English thoroughbred horse was of no value to run races for money, it was necessary to dispose of him at some price. His physical adaptability and high-strung nervous organization rendered him unfit for the yeoman, so he was put to stage-coach uses; but here he was unmanageable, except with a rider upon his back, and as his only gait was to run, the necessary riders were now termed or named postilions.

As the wars diminished in Europe, and greater attention was given to agriculture, the people demanded horses fit for that work; hence draught-horses had to be produced, but the thoroughbred running-horse could not be moulded into adaptability for such uses.

The first crosses down from it were necessarily mongrel, and were termed "cock-tails" or "quarter-horses." The next remove down were branded with the created appellation of "dung-hills," that they might be forever discarded by the nobility; and this is the class of horses our sporting-paper writers continually harp upon as the only class of horses fit for the American gentleman's coach or road-wagon,—*i.e.*, the English nobility's discarded "dung-hills." Such writers certainly cannot know these truths, or they would not so advocate.

The Arabian blood, I have said, was plastic to mould into any form or type. This people did not know; hence looked about for horses to answer their purposes for work whose build should be suitable, and whose temper would be quiet and tractable. With mongrelization comes cold blood and grossness of flesh, also softness of bone and dull intellect. Men think beef or grossness of flesh means strength; strength comes with nerve-power; and as we improve the animal in blood, the muscle becomes more firm and hard, the bone smaller, but more dense, and the nerve-power gives greater strength, even to the do or die qualities desired. No other horse can endure, for an equal length of time and upon low diet, what the thoroughbred Arabian can. Cromwell and the "Roundheads" had taken many Arabian horses into Scotland to be bred down, and from these came the Clydesdale. The Flanders horse was brought into England, and by degrees they bred into a class of horses suitable for the demands of the English people; not knowing, however, what bloods were accountable for the animal now so useful to them. The thoroughbred running-horse lost its value to the masses, becoming a toy for the nobility, of great expense, which only the very wealthy had use for; and that use was running races for a pastime in their idleness, and for chance or gambling. Grades from the thoroughbred running-horse were less vicious and excitable, so were adapted to fox-hunts and other great sport for the nobility; and from a still lower grade was formed the "Cleveland Bay," a self-sustaining type, but unable, of its own mongrelized blood, to create other more valuable horses. This "Cleveland Bay" is called the English coach-horse, and there he stops, as a non-producer of other desirable types.

In France a few wealthy noblemen, with the breeder's gift, imported Arabian stallions and mares, from which experiments were tried in a new climate, and upon different soil, with better and more abundant feed. Without knowledge, their efforts were of no special results; but with experiment came information. Fresh Arabs were imported, among them Godolphin Arabian and Gallipoli. These two Arabian stallions were bred on to now native (in France) Arabian blood, upon the principle of "once out and thrice back to a primitive blood," and the horse of the country became known as La Perche, later the Norman Percheron.

Godolphin Arabian went to England to be the getter of the best running-horses they had up to his day, because he reinforced his own blood; but coming through French ownership as he did, with English national pride, they for a time ignored Godolphin Arabian, trying to fix their type as purely "national," by saying their own importations were the factors, and their Darley Arabian the cause.

However, the blood of Godolphin Arabian left in La Perche in sons and daughters, uniting with affinity blood of Gallipoli in sons and daughters (once out and thrice back), made a strong foundation before the French breeders were aware of it for their now beautiful national horse, the "Percheron." (Please refer to the French government statistics gathered and contributed by the veteran author Charles Du Hays, also by Mons. Fardouet.)

Intelligent and gifted men like Du Hays and Fardouet encouraged close breeding of the type now founded, and the result of such close relationships has given them a horse demanded the world over where draught-horses are wanted, while the demand for the English race-horse is limited to the sporting fraternity, either of the nobility or the lower grades who live by gambling.

It is not so many years, after all, since these two families of "national horses" were created and established. The possibilities in man are very great where concerted action is taken; but, unfortunately, one-half of man's life is spent in discord and opposition. Every man has an opinion, thinking *he* knows best; or, finding he does not know, dislikes to yield; and if he has an abundance of means will, from no laudable motives, devote all his capital with his energies to kill the object which he knows will mortify his pride, especially when he can see and know that success is bound to come with the superior man, of

low financial estate, who has presumed to know more than himself. Again, certain classes of journalists are a fearful obstacle to rapid progress. They are but weather-cocks of public opinion; but, being men, are warped by the almighty dollar, with neither information nor interest at stake upon success or failure of any great enterprise beyond, as I have said, the money for their pen and type to themselves.

I have said enough about the English race-horse to have shown that he is of Arabian origin, and of no value except to run races. To breed him up, or to sustain his vitality, no blood can be introduced but his own primitive blood of the Arabian. To breed him down, makes the English nobility's "dung-hill," or American gentleman's road- and coach-horse, for such as like to ride behind them.

I have abundantly shown that both the English race-horse and the French Percheron were created by man from the God horse, or Arabian. It is no sacrilege to say God's horse, for *He* made the Arabian, from which man made the mongrels.

Let us now go to Russia and inquire into their national horse. It is called the "Russian Orloff trotting-horse." This horse should be an argument for the American people. Russia, like America, is a vast territory, and has use for general purpose horses such as have speed at the trotting gait and can endure for long distances. They, too, as a people, wanted what they had not got for work purposes, and particularly the road. They tried the English running-horse, only to prove to themselves, as have we, that he was of no good except to run races.

It seems unfortunate that individuals should be called upon to fight, single-handed, battles for important improvements through rediscoveries or inventions, but that is God's will.

To Count Alexis Orloff is due the Russian trotting-horse bearing his name. The count imported an Arabian stallion, and by him created a type, through in-and-in breeding after his first out-cross. Do not understand by *first out-cross* as one single get, but from selections from all the get by one horse out of differently bred mares. Thus, Count Orloff used Danish mares of low type and English running mares, that blood being at that time strongly the affinity or Arabian blood.

At the time of Count Orloff's death he had a family of thoroughbred trotting-bred horses, which the people had learned to value so highly that the government purchased the entire collection late in the forties, or in 1845.

Up to the time of the count's death he would sell no stallion, feeling that in order to create the type pure and to be recognized as strictly thoroughbred it must be under one man's control, or until so numerous and fixed in its type as to remain so. In that particular I can sympathize with Count Orloff. I will here speak of my individual self in my attempts. Men knowing the burden I was financially carrying, and desiring to help me without putting their hands into their own pockets, would urge me to sell, bringing friends to buy the very choicest of my stock, which had just reached an age for reproduction, and which, being close bred to purification, were my life in the enterprise. Such gentlemen, while they intended well, would ruin me through an uninformed attempt to assist, or become angry because I would not destroy, as they suggested, through sale.

After the imperial government of Russia had purchased the Count Orloff family,—now sufficiently numerous to produce liberally,—they continued to hold annual sales of young or surplus stock, the government being surety for purity in blood and breeding.

For interesting information upon this question I refer the reader to Mr. A. J. Rousseau's publication upon the methods pursued by Count Orloff in breeding and founding this justly-celebrated "national trotting-, road-, and coach-horse." This horse is so bred, and is so intensely Arabian, that, like imported Messenger (which was three times inbred to the Godolphin Arabian), it will cross with any class of horses, improving the family it is crossed upon.

The Orloff is himself a superior coach-horse, an untiring stagehorse, and a whirlwind of trotting speed for road or sporting purposes.

During our Grand Central Circuit Meeting (trotting), a few years since, some, then recently imported, Orloff stallions were exhibited upon the track here at Rochester, New York. I examined them carefully in the boxes, and found them the counterpart of old Andrew Jackson and his best son, Henry Clay. In physical conformation they were identical with the get of Jackson and Clay, also in color and disposition. When shown at speed upon our track, I heard many farmers remark that it was a fraud to show them as Russian horses, for they were only Clays!

I have now introduced the reader to three typical "national horses," each one representing a nation independent and powerful in resources and wealth, also advanced in the arts and sciences from cultured and refined civilization. Each nation had resorted to the Arabian horse from which to create; and, with national pride or independence, no one had obtained his foundation from the mongrelizations of the other, but had taken the primitive God-made animal, that all honor and glory should come to Him, the eternal ruler of the universe.

Ward's Science Shops, at Rochester, New York, hold a front place before all the scientific world. They are near me, and I often resort to them for study. One old man, Professor Ballay (a Frenchman), has for fifty years been handling bones as an osteologist; indeed, we may say, he has lived among the skeletons of the animal kingdom since a boy, passing through the first shops and schools in Germany, France, and England to these of Professor Henry A. Ward, of Rochester.

From him I learned much. His familiarity with the bony anatomy of the animal kingdom was such that at sight he could tell almost any bone handed to him, to what animal or species of animal, and in what part of the frame, it belonged.

My library took in Darwin, Huxley, Proctor, and Tyndall, all of whom I had studied, but had put to one side as of very highly-cultured imaginations. The facts of life, of death, or creation, they failed to reach.

Old Ballay was quite profane at times, so I asked him one day if he believed there was a God. "Most certainly!" he replied. "Do you believe in the teachings of the Bible?" I asked him. "Yes, sir; I do," was his answer. I now asked him what he thought of Darwin, Huxley, and Proctor. "Well," he answered, "I think Mr. Darwin fancied he was a great man when he was young, but as he grew older, and found what a fool he had been in much of his writings, he thought he would go on and see how many and how great fools he could make of other men." Of evolution, the old man said, it could never stop. "If animal life owed its varieties to evolution, changes would be continuous; but here I have been dissecting and mounting skeletons for fifty years, and have seen skeletons that were a thousand years old, and every time the bones were the same in the different animals to which they belonged. The same was the case in the human skeleton. If anything in life was of spontaneous growth, it would continue to change; if the different families were results of crosses out of positive families, sporting back to one or the other of original types would be a necessary result, and the bony anatomy would first detect the started change, if there were any in *structure*. On the contrary, it was ever the same over and over again, just as God first made it. Then again, abrupt crosses produced life, but the new life being a violation of God's laws could not reproduce itself." Ballay's workshop had been with the dead, but his thoughts had been of life.

Of domestic families he spoke of the high type and the low. The bones in each told of the blood and breeding of the animal. The high types were nearest to God's creation, but the low types of mongrelization spoke of man's ignorance, were soft and porous.

The more the animal was mongrelized the softer and more porous the bones became, also larger than in the foundation type. Mr. Ballay was no horseman, nor was he in any way interested in them, nor did he know of the different names of horses; but he cited the two skeletons he had mounted for the Smithsonian Institution at Washington. One was of the thoroughbred Lexington, the other of Old Henry Clay. The first had been removed from the flesh, not subject to decomposition; the latter, of Old Henry Clay, had been subject to fourteen years' burial in the ground. He had cleaned, prepared, and mounted both, and pronounced those of Henry Clay as from the best-bred animal, being finer, more dense, and of an elastic character peculiar to the highest bred animal. Those of Lexington were dense but brittle, showing inferior blood and breeding. When I introduce the Arabian origin of Old Henry Clay, I will let the intelligent student reason it out. Self-teaching is the most effective. I am a self-convicted believer in the Bible and in God, as I also know Mr. Henry M. Stanley to have been. The more I studied into animal life, the more I became interested in Bible history, seeking it for information I could nowhere else obtain. The deeper I went, the more insignificant the scientific works I possessed (treating upon such subjects) became.

I have told the reader a little of what I knew of the breedings from the Arabian horse by other civilized countries, and what they got; now it has seemed to me that we, as a young country, should learn from the old and more experienced. They have proved what can and what cannot be done. I was always ready to listen to the old that I might learn from their experience, and improve if possible upon them. Now that I am old, who of the young will take up where I leave off?

America is a young country, and far from being as old as were these three great countries named, before they settled upon the different types of horses now recognized as their national horse; moreover, no one of these countries found within themselves the blood from which to create these types; but each one went to Egypt or Arabia for the primitive horse, for on no other spot upon the face of the globe could it be found, except the country where God's word had been given to man, and at which place names were given to all created animal life.

Why was it that these three great nations went to Arabia for this horse from which to create new types? If Mr. Darwin were alive, I wonder if he could explain this question better than does Bible history? From no other horse could these three families be produced, nor can either of them produce other new, desirable, self-sustaining types.

As I have said, the reader must now become his own teacher, and if he be a deep thinker and condensed reasoner, he will grow strong in his opinions.

Again for our own country,—America! We found wild horses here called Indian ponies. Could we create anything from them? No; we imported from our mother-country, and from Arabia and Egypt, Persia and Turkey, as well as France and England, over fifty Arabian and barb stallions. Beside these, there were brought a great many English thoroughbred running-horses, close to the Arabian blood.

This was between 1760 and 1835, since when, or from 1835 up to the breaking out of the war in 1861, we had at intervals quite a number more; so that with the beginning of the war no country had such uniformly good horses as America; and yet, we as a people paid no attention to their breeding. For years "two-forty down the plank" was in every boy's mouth, for all our horses trotted, and the best of coach-horses were plenty and cheap.

The trotting-tracks had not been recognized as an institution to be sustained and supported by fashionable wealth. Our vehicles were heavy, and harness more so. The shoeing of our horses was primitive; and when I look at the big, coarse, heavy shoes of Old Henry Clay, as compared with the delicately-finished shoe of to-day, and those spikes for nails by the side of the little finished Putnam nail, I ask what made our old-time horses trot so fast and endure so much without training or condition. The reply comes, "Blood and breeding." What blood? The Arabian, which had permeated the blood of most of our horses in our new and then almost unextended civilization. Our horses were centred in the Eastern States, where the Arabian blood of Messenger was well diffused, and frequently reinforced by primitive blood from the occasionally imported Arabian; yet none of these Arabian horses had been used to any extent except in New England, New York State, New Jersey, Maryland, Virginia, and Kentucky; still, all were used, and "blood would tell."

In New England they had Arabian blood direct, in their Morgan horse; also more or less Messenger descendants, so that New England and New York State were famous for good horses.

Our dreadful war began in the spring of 1861, calling for large numbers of horses. The cause was one that interested every man, so that if he could not give himself, he gave of horses the best he had. Many and many were the horses I saw given by the farmers in this country for seventy-five to one hundred dollars, which six months before they would have refused to sell to me for three hundred dollars, as to a horse-dealer for market; but they gave cheerfully at any price named by the government, thinking to help the country.

Up to this period our importations had been very limited; restricted almost to thoroughbred race-horses, with at great intervals an Arabian or two. The race-horses were to reinforce Kentucky's thoroughbreds, while Arabians were usually presents to our Presidents from the Egyptian or Turkish empires.

Our war increased in magnitude, and horses became scarce. Resort was had to Canada; we also brought from Texas, New Mexico, and the far West, large numbers of *mustangs*: indeed anything that would wear a harness and draw a plough or a load, was pressed into service. Many farmers exchanged works, thus making one or two pairs of horses do the labor upon three farms. In 1864 an uncle of my wife (Mr. John W. Taylor, of East Bloomfield, Ontario County, New York, who bought the third colt from Flora Temple's dam for the late R. A. Alexander, of Kentucky), who was himself suffering for horses upon his farm, went to Texas and New Mexico, bringing home one hundred and forty head of mustang-horses of all ages. They were stallions and mares, unbroken; but as I have said, horses were so scarce that anything would do, and these one hundred and forty head of mustangs were soon scattered among the farmers in the county, valued at that time, but cursed in memory to-day, both in themselves and produce, for all were bred that would breed. Now it is twenty years past, and why has not the produce proved other than a waste of time and money through breeding it? The Canada mares had been so mongrelized by all grades of horses—the English thoroughbred, the English shire or draught-horse, the Clyde and half-bred Percherons—that such mares as came from Canada and were bred, proved but a trifle better than the mustangs as producers; of course, Canada did not sell us her best.

Capital, always looking for investments, saw money in the importing of good work-horses; so the thoroughbred Percheron draught-horse and the Scotch Clyde were brought in by sample lots. To-day, the importation of these horses is considered one of the most profitable investments by the importer; but is it treating our agriculturists fairly? Is it justice to our farmers, burdened as we are with our war-debt? Every reader knows that we are one of the greatest grass lands in the world, and that the area in which these imported horses are grown would not make the extent of grass land comprised in any one of our forty States and Territories. If our sporting and agricultural papers had given themselves to instructing their readers during the past twenty years, we could have created, grown, and established a national horse of our own, equal if not superior to anything we now import, and would be able to sell the same animals to any part of Europe for one-half of what we now pay for them, besides making all the profit from our grass lands by such raising, which we now pay out to Europe in hard dollars.

Another disadvantage we have labored under: a sporting nature had grown and been cultivated by our young men during the war, which settled largely on trotting-horses. The demand for trotters was great, with prospective large returns from their breeding. Hundreds of gentlemen of means, but in every other way unfitted, purchased land and began the breeding of horses.

Brood stock was selected by prejudice or fancy, without cultured ability for understandingly investigating the reputed breedings, through which to rate blood influences for desired results. In short, the *name* was the governing power, blood and breeding being of minor importance.

Horses of all classes were exceedingly scarce, and the demand was so great that venturers in breeding, in haste to get rich, thought more of prospective large money returns from their investments than of future advantages to the country through improved blood values. Prejudice swayed the breeding and buying public, so that after twenty-five years of unparalleled production of horses, as to numbers, we find the country flooded with mongrels, scarce worth the raising, and from which we are unable to select a reliable, self-sustaining, reproducing type.

Our constant importation of stock-horses from France, Scotland, England, and even German-Prussia, has not mended matters, but has still further mongrelized our bloods, because we have used them for *crosses*, rather than in breeding each type to itself.

If the different horses we continue to import have special merit to warrant such importations, why not breed them pure; then with our superior advantages in soil and climate, eclipse our cis-Atlantic neighbors in the growing of their own types? Poor America! When will she arise to the privilege and dignity of breeding her own national horse?

Journal advocates of a *name*, seeing the mistake they had made in so strongly sympathizing with public prejudice in favor of that *name*, now began to print "cross and out-cross," which was soon taken up by the people, who wanted to know what they should "cross and out-cross" with? This was soon fixed for another deal, and the theory of thoroughbred running-horse blood was blazoned on the "out-cross" banner. By using it, the broken-down race-horse stallions, also weeds from that type, would be got rid of among the unsuspecting yeomanry, only however to entail another drawback to successful breeding of a "national horse;" and thus the attempt by a single individual for good general results, became a most stupendous undertaking. However, my faith was great, for *I did know;* and the resolve being made, I did *begin;* believing there were plenty of men in the country who would co-operate with me in this attempt.

Kentucky had a great prestige in her brood mares, and sporting journals harped the string, "cross and out-cross," urging the use of broken-down thoroughbred running-horses as stallions.

That others valued Arabian blood as I did was evident from occasional importations of it; but in no case can I remember their use being credited. From 1840 to 1860 I knew of quite a number so imported, two standing at Boston, three in New Jersey, three in Maryland, two in Virginia, and four in Kentucky.

From the first, Arabian stallions worked into Kentucky, where they were used upon race-horse mares. Latterly, Mokhladi, Massaud, and Sacklowie, imported by the late A. Keene Richards into Kentucky, did more or less business upon all kinds of dams, as well as thoroughbred running-breds. I am willing to believe the public did not know, in truth, the value of Arabian blood in the coach-, road-, and trotting-horse as well as race-horse.

When, however, credit is given to Kentucky for superior blood in her *brood* mares over any other State, and that superiority is credited to her thorough running-horse blood, which in an earlier day was the only type of horses she bred, we are inclined to look for a more direct *cause*. In doing so, we find that for forty years their dams have been under the influence of Arabian blood; no less than five different Arabian stallions having been imported directly into Kentucky since 1850. While these horses were obtained expressly to reinforce their running-horse blood, when they found it more important to breed general-purpose horses (as coach-, road-, trotting-horses and workers), they had the all-important Arabian blood to help them, whether to strengthen running or colder-bred mares. Now, in so writing of Kentucky, I will cite one single instance—of which I have many—showing the direct and positive value of Arabian blood in the coach- and trotting-horse. In 1854, Mr. L. L. Dorsey, of Kentucky, bred a daughter of the imported Arabian Zilcaadie to a little inbred Morgan horse called Vermont Morgan. The get and produce was called Golddust, from his golden color. This colt, foaled in 1855, was bred upon the principle of once out and thrice back to a primitive blood, for Justin Morgan was Arabian-bred.

The horse Vermont Morgan was but fourteen and three-quarters hands high, and was inbred to Justin Morgan's blood. Now, when he is put to the daughter of imported *Zilcaadie*, one of the most beautiful stallion colts known in this country was the result; I mean L. L. Dorsey's stallion Golddust. He grew to be sixteen hands high, weighing very nearly thirteen hundred pounds, and for trotting speed was the peer of anything before bred in Kentucky. "He was trotted many races, never being beaten; one of them was a match race for ten thousand dollars, which he won by over a distance."

As a getter, Golddust was the most positive sire for beauty, size, and wonderful trotting speed in his colts, calling to mind Andrew Jackson, similarly bred, also imported Messenger of similar breeding. It makes me nearly wild as I write, that I cannot induce men to put away prejudice and use reason. I do not wish the reader to obey my teachings, but would beg of every man interested in the breeding of horses to think deep, embracing every opportunity to enlighten himself. We have already too many writers who demand their readers to do as they say in print; I simply urge men to be better informed of themselves.

Such a crop of colts as were the first get by Mr. Dorsey's Arabian-bred horse had no parallel in the breeding of beautiful coach-, road-, and trotting-horses, except in the get of imported Messenger, Andrew Jackson, and his son Henry Clay, all three being similarly bred to Arabian blood influence. Moreover, these sons and daughters of Dorsey's old Golddust had the same high nervous temperament possessed by the get of Andrew Jackson and Henry Clay, also credited to the get of imported Messenger.

If I write too much, men will not read; if I say too little, they will not understand. Men never trouble themselves to condemn and abuse what is of no value, or what they fully understand; but will bring all their forces in wealth and prejudice to destroy what beats them or stands in their way, not stopping to study into the values of the obstacles.

I have been charged with being over-enthusiastic in the matter of Arabian blood, called by us Clay. Now, I never began to contend for it as did Mr. Weaver of Philadelphia, or Mr. Dorsey of Kentucky, for each of these gentlemen contended for their individual horse. My contention has been for the blood, *pro bono publico;* and even in that particular I was misjudged by friends, who would ask me "if it was glory" I was after. Far from it.

In the matter of Golddust, the war broke out, and his possibilities for Kentucky and the country at large were cut short. I remember a lot of horses and mares by Golddust, which Mr. Dorsey sent on to Long Island at the beginning of the war. They were in a large barn near John I. Sneidicker's place, near the old Union track. I examined them many times, and will say that to-day, such *good* horses are *rare*. After the war, attempts to establish Golddust were frustrated from two causes: first was owing to the multitude of coarse horses, more fashionable in the name, and second was the mistaken idea of improving the blood of Golddust through infusion of the blood of the rigid running-horse with its instinct. Had Mr. Dorsey selected inbred Morgan and high-type Clay mares for his horse he would by this time have created a "national coach-, road-, and trotting-horse" without equal in the world. The same could have been accomplished with Messenger, or with Young Bashaw, or Andrew Jackson, or Henry Clay. The opportunities for a "national horse" have presented themselves, but have not been embraced because of want of intelligent application to the object upon the part of gentlemen of means. General William T. Withers, of Kentucky, is now working towards such a base. I know him to be creating a superior maternal foundation, but whether he will introduce the right form of blood in the male, remains to be seen.

Naturally, he will feel pride in establishing his breed through his Almont; and while Almont did possess largely of Arabian blood through Andrew Jackson and Pilot, and the maternal foundation will be solid through "Clay" and Keene Richards's Arab mares, his results would be more uniform and every way more satisfactory, were he to make the king of his haras a direct descendant of a high-type Arabian stallion, through a Morgan, Jackson, or a Clay mare; but small mistakes by the individual have disappointed more than one Napoleonic attempt. The General remembers that by *the male* are the names given; and that rich mother-earth grows poor seed into prominence. Such seed, however, must be sustained by always rich mother-earth, for renewed vitality. God's laws are perfect; man cannot improve upon them. Atavism, or *sporting* back, is more apt to come through the blood influence of the dam than of the sire. I will soon speak particularly of that.

But why did I breed to General Grant's Arabs, you ask?

When I have asked a man why he bred a *mustang*, his reply was, For fun! Was there any sense in the act or in the reply?

To this time I have been placing the argument so that reason within the reader would answer the question.

When William H. Seward's Arabians arrived in 1860 (now twenty-five years ago), I had quite a little information upon blood and breeding of horses,—more, indeed, than some men ever will have; but as it is very unprofitable information, I trust all young men will not be so foolish as I have been. However, I was in the boat, so had to keep paddling and stopping the leaks at the same time; and here I am to-day, barely afloat: I know, however, there is a safe harbor for me at the end.

We learn of great facts through deep problems, slowly. It takes time. Thorough investigations are very difficult.

From 1820 to 1860 I believed I had made a careful inquiry and investigation into such Arabian stallions, with results, as had been imported to America to the date of arrival of the late Mr. Seward's horses; but the war was under way, stopping, for the time, all else.

Later, as a dealer and still experimental breeder, the question of Secretary Seward's Arabian horses came up, and my search for them proved like most others of the kind: they had been thrown away. What was left to show for them was being credited to "time-standard bred horses;" thus, the two best colts to date by one celebrated "time-standard" bred horse, are from a granddaughter of the only son of one of Seward's Arabian horses, out of a granddaughter of Old Henry Clay: which facts are not known, so the time-standard bred horse gets all credit for the two mares got by him.

Up to the time of the arrival of General Grant's Arabians I could find no record of the attempts by any man or men to create, with intent and purpose, any specialty from the Arabian horse, while my investigations warranted an effort, as my writings have shown.

Russia and America demand coach-, stage-, and road-horses to a greater extent than any other nation; and they must be of a class adapted to general-purpose uses.

Russia has created and established her national horse upon that base of trotting instinct, and I have shown she did it upon the same

Arabian blood used by England and France for their separate, distinctive national horses.

I have also shown that our most positive and valuable horses for the road or sporting uses, were the more closely related to Arabian blood.

One of our drawbacks from progress as a nation in all scientific studies is the want of means by the individual, and the pellmell rush of every man to get rich. Money, money, money, is the tocsin for every lad, or man; or, "Is there any money it?" "Is there any money in it?" Our country is too fast; the corners of the fences are not cultivated, when in them are acres of the richest land.

"Haste is waste." I was prepared for the arrival of General Grant's Arabs. I believed, as will any American, that they must be of the highest possible type. No empire or nation would insult itself by presenting to so great a man, also the one representative man of so great a nation as ours, an inferior gift from its representative animal life. General Grant's Arabs had to be the purest and best.

The best results obtained by any crosses are not through abrupt, but by affinity crosses, with the instinct bending in the way you want. The Arab being plastic, reinforces a high type of man's creation by its more vitalizing blood. To breed it to the race-horse, makes that blood hotter and stouter in its instinct established; and so with any other high forms of man's creation. Bread is not flour, nor is flour wheat; and yet except for the wheat there would be neither flour, bread, cake, nor pie. So in breeding; there must be the wheat, the seed; the life. In horses it is the Arabian seed, blood, and life from which man can create.

I have implied that extreme physical conformations and developments, with rigid instincts as created by man, are very difficult to change.

We wanted a national horse of a type which should conform itself to our greatest demands; which were stage, coach, road, and for track uses as trotters.

We could not afford to mould over the running-horse to such purposes; indeed, time and money have proven it too uncertain.

We had the trotting instinct already moulded to a type we wanted; what we needed was to build this type up to a degree of superiority; and the only way was to reinforce it with fresh, pure blood from the *cause,—i.e.*, Arabian blood; this General Grant had been sent from abroad in his two Arabian stallions, and he offered it to his people.

Upon their arrival the only blood we had adapted for good, prompt results, was that of Henry Clay. Its physical and instinctive organs would assimilate more readily than that of any other type of horses we had, because of itself purer in the primitive blood. It came nearer to Sir Thomas Morton's saying of three hundred years ago, "Once out and thrice back to a primitive blood for best results."

When the general's horses arrived, I had two daughters of Old Henry Clay: both were got by him when he was owned in Monroe County, near Rochester, New York. One was a brood mare, being bred to a son of Henry Clay, her half-brother. I wanted virgin mares to send to General Grant's horses, if I could find them.

I secured two young mares, coming four and five, in Michigan, in 1880. They were own sisters, by Jack Sheppard by Henry Clay, out of his (Jack's) own daughter. The next best son of Henry Clay was Colonel Wadsworth, bred by the late William W. Wadsworth, who owned Henry Clay. This stallion, with one of his own daughters, went to Nashville, Tennessee. I went there, and, although the stallion was dead, found four of his daughters, aged at the time from two to seven (coming three to eight); the youngest being by him from his own daughter. I took this filly with the two best of the other three. *The two* Mr. Jewett had, but the little filly I put one side with the two Sheppard fillies and one daughter of Henry Clay. I next went to New York City and bought back a young mare I had sold there the fall before for seven hundred and fifty dollars, as a road mare, allowing fifteen hundred dollars for her. She was bred near Rochester, New York, and was by Red Bird by Henry Clay, out of an inbred Morgan mare. I now had five young, sound, healthy, virgin mares by Henry Clay, or by his sons, three being inbred, and all were choice; four being very fast natural trotters, and the fifth one would be were she not mixed at times in her gait.

All this had been done in the fall, winter, and spring of 1879 and 1880, Grant's horses arriving in the summer of 1879.

These mares I considered up to the English standard of blood and breeding.

Permit me to explain my reason for selecting virgin mares for General Grant's stallions. I have shown that I desired blood akin, well bred, and possessed of as much consanguinity as possible.

Forty years ago, while a young man, I bred fine dogs, game-cocks, and fancy pigeons. From early boyhood I had bred small pets, studying quite a little into life as related to them.

I used to be much with old cockers in those days, to learn of them what was interesting to me.

I may be mistaken, but I am under the impression they were a stronger and better type of men than we now find in that class. They were mostly those who had been *heelers* and *handlers* for such of the English nobility, as were more given to those sports then, than at the present day, consequently better informed from contact. Nearly fifty years ago I had a beautiful setter bitch. An old English cocker whom I called frequently to see, was always in a worry for fear some cur or mongrel dog would get with her, and was worried, saying that if such an accident were to happen, she would forever after be worthless for breeding purposes. The only reason he could give me was that any puppies she might subsequently have would be "dung-hills," even by the best-bred dog. (The word "dung-hill" is unpleasant to write or to speak, but is the only word used to express extreme contempt among the class of men, of high or low degree, interested in the breeding of sporting animals.)

The same injunction was made relative to my game-hens and a cold-bred cock; or my black-and-tan dogs, fearing a cur cross.

From boyhood I wanted a reason for everything. Words that I did not understand, I wanted so thoroughly explained that I could use them properly myself. The statements by this old cocker I found to be the fixed opinion with all men of his class, but no one could explain them to me. However, there was so much common sense with these men (then fifty to sixty years old, now fifty years ago, which would make them over one hundred if alive), that their "say so" made an impression upon me, for they were always possessed of the breeder's gift, which should be observing to a fine degree. Moreover, their contact with their intelligent employers in the old country had tended to orally educate them into many important problems relating to breeding; so I, too, learned from them, or was pushed to inform myself.

The older I grew, the more impressive the opinions of these men became; and as I continued a student in animal life, I have learned to listen with respect to the teachings of old men of strong minds, whether illiterate or slightly educated; thus, whether cock-fighters, dog-fighters, or pugilists. I have found there was something to be learned from all, or each; and here let me say that a capable man in either one of these low occupations is almost invariably a man of superiority, mentally; all he requires to make him a recognized man, is the restraining influences of education with association. I never knew an able one to be a drunkard.

This all-powerful first blood influence upon the virgin female, was a saying with these old men that must have a reason. As breeders of game-cocks and bull-dogs they had listened, observed, and verified to their satisfaction.

The illiterate man is the best-informed man in the world so far as he goes, because he tests and proves what he cannot reason out through reading and study.

My inquiring mind would not rest until I could test, or in some way precipitate this saying by these men. I hunted over all the books I could get upon breeding, but in no place could I find the subject treated; so I tested it in thoroughbred black-and-tan dogs and in game-cocks, until I said Amen! it is so. To test blood influences, one must resort to small things of early maturity.—man's life is short.

Later on, my position was such that almost nightly I listened to such men as old Dr. Mott, the late Willard Parker, Dr. Simms, and men of great research in the medical world as relates to life in man; also was much in the New York hospitals, always a listener and thinker, as well as student.

I learned that few men were gifted in their professions; many adopted a profession, but few had the calling.

In those days we had much consumption and scrofula among the young and middle-aged. It was a constant study and subject for discussion with these then young physicians. That scrofula and consumption were inherited was asserted; but what was *the cause*, was the point of study before treatment could be successful.

Young mothers would often die of consumption after bearing one or two children, and the children would grow up scrofulous, to die in the end of consumption.

In many instances these young mothers had been known as strong, healthy girls, from strong, healthy parents, and the inherent cause was imagined to be in some remote relative.

Men forget to quote, "The sins of the fathers shall be visited upon the children unto the third and fourth generation," or, "Be sure your sin will find you out." No man or woman can violate God's law without entailing a penalty.

Through my interest in breeding, in connection with other occupation associated with life, I could never get over the feeling that there must have been at some time printed matter upon the question advanced to me by these old cockers of fifty years ago, as to after-results from first conceptions, and which saying has been continued with them to the present day. If there were a cause for physical entailment of disease in man, it must be of a similar cause for influence upon the virgin brute through a first conception, for subsequent conceptions to different males. Reproduction of life in man, is the same as with the brute; and as everything pertaining to *life* is of importance to man, there should be no restraint upon a proper discussion of such topic.

The seed is life in man or beast; it is blood. If we sow wheat that is diseased, the crop will be diseased. If we plant smut corn, our field will yield abundantly of smut corn. And so in the vegetable kingdom, disease produces disease in the following crops. Life is life, whether vegetable, animal, or human; and man was intended to study himself, through observation and comparison; with life largely subjected to his will. The ground is mother-earth, and can become diseased so as to bring forth diseased fruit. It partakes of the first seed planted in it, to contribute in succeeding births, health or disease.

Constitutional imperfections in the male may be absorbed by the female, to be given out again and again in her produce to different males.

Although I had proven to myself thirty years ago, that the influence of the first male upon the system of the female was such that she gave of her constitutional impregnation to the get of other males, I still continued to search in old medical and scientific works for some treatise upon the question.

I had reasoned the matter out within myself, but wanted other authority than my own by way of verification, and at last found it; but must repeat from memory. Although precisely my own conclusions, I will not say to the reader, I am the man.

Let every reader and every thinker remember that there is nothing new under the sun, not even in the mind of man.

One day, while in the office of a physician gifted in obstetrics and female diseases or disorders, I found in his library a very old medical and scientific work, dated in England in 1700, with extracts dating in 1600. In it, the very subject which for so many years I had studied over, was treated upon; and opened to me the origin of the old English cocker's saying of fifty years ago. The article was entitled, "The Influence of the Blood of the Male upon the Female in After-conceptions by Different Males," and reasoned thus:

First, the seed is life. In animal or human it is blood, but life: seed first, blood second, then life.

Here let me illustrate to such as will understand. Life is in the seed, which may be at a high or low degree. To *diminish the seed*, is to lower vitality or vigor of life.

With many living things, coition between the sexes is certain death to the male. He has given *his seed, his life.* This I learned in 1835 while breeding and growing silk-worms. The most beautiful and vigorous millers would come from the cocoons, and after one coition, death was certain to the male, while the female lived on to lay her eggs. To take the male and confine him alone, was to lengthen his life with continued vigor; but the laws of re-creation demanded death through the giving of life. I will continue from this treatise of 1600:

The seed of the male is life; if life, it is blood; and the *blood* is what is recognized as of importance in the breeding of animals.

The virgin we will suppose to be as she usually is, pure as sunlight, in her blood, to one type (for we are not now doing with mongrels, only as we create them).

Coition takes place between the male and a virgin female. The seed is received into the uterus or womb, where it germinates into blood, which, united with that of the virgin, becomes part of her life, fed by her blood. Now, if this fœtus be in truth a part of the male, then the life of his seed must contribute to the life of the growing fœtus. The blood of the growing fœtus, representing both sire and mother, passes back and forth with each pulsation of the heart of the mother, through her entire system, feeding and replenishing her system to all draughts upon it during the period of gestation, or up to maturity of and birth of the foal. Now, if we say the new-born foal partakes of the blood of the sire, and that blood has to a certain extent been feeding the system of its mother for a period of eleven months, we have a right to suppose that the blood of the sire of the new-born foal still remains in the system of the virgin dam; and from it, she must impart to her next foal by some other horse. If this be not so, then it makes no difference what the blood of the dam may be, so long as the sire is all right; but such reasoning as this would be against *human* reason; or, if I am correct, then we have an explanation of *atavism,* or *sporting* back. With me the argument is a fact; and is one that should draw attention from all breeders. More study with deeper thinking is what is needed, and less "*cross* and *cut-cross*" business.

It is supposed that the nerve-power is mostly given by the dam; but that is a blind supposition. If the dam be the better bred of the two, as was usually the case when the well-bred Clay mare was prostituted to colder blood, then she did contribute most of the nerve-power for speed to the foal; but breed any kind of a mare one may prefer, to a thoroughbred Arabian horse, and they will find the nerve-power will be given by the horse to the foal, thus proving again that "blood will tell."

Animals should be bred to one blood instinct in order to be getters of a positive type; not the desired instinct *in one*, with a belief that it will predominate over a deficiency in the other, and that the produce will be superior to either sire or dam. The talk about building up this *deficiency*, or reducing a surplus of some one propensity through this cross or that cross, is the most astonishing talk to me, from otherwise intelligent men.

For success in breeding, both male and female must be true to one type; then with united effort, the young is improved. Messenger was a great getter, because the blood of both sire and dam was close to the one original type,—Godolphin Arabian.

The experience of Thomas Bates in breeding short-horns, illustrates the importance of purity of blood to one type, in both male and female. The repeated destruction of the foundation for the English thoroughbred running-horse, through external and internal wars between 1639 and 1700, with every time a resort to original or primitive blood of the Arabian, should be a lesson to all not to be much blinded by prejudice.

OF EXTENDED PEDIGREES.

It is customary to extend the pedigree of horses back as far as possible. No thought is given to the blood influence, simply a desire to reach at some point back, a prominent thoroughbred running-horse.

Thus, in such pedigrees we find bloods that were *supposed* to pace; others which were known to be mongrel-bred running-horses, with a work-horse or two; but in the end, Diomed or Messenger are certain to be added, to whom to credit all good.

All through these long lines of ancestry we find mongrel-bred horses; but every time a running-bred horse is found or made to fit, the enthusiastic prejudiced advocate of race-horse blood, points his finger with pride to the printers' ink, of *the name*,—not the blood instinct, for it is not there except to *run*, were the animal alive.

Now, for the benefit of such uninformed but visionary advocates of Diomed blood influences, let me state how he was bred, when he was foaled, and when he died, then tell me what possible blood influence he can have upon any horse of to-day; or, better, we will say that he did stud duty in the State of Virginia from 1799 to 1807, and that he was twenty-two years old when first covering a mare in Virginia. Of course, from twenty-two to twenty-nine were his years of stud service, and in all my experience with old horses I have never known of one to be a very sure foal-getter, except for a very limited number of mares, when past twenty-three years old. Diomed got but few, and of course they were running-bred of different breedings, which meant dilution of his blood influences, except to the one instinct—run, which was the all-absorbing thought in breeding in Virginia,—*i.e.*, to win at the running gait.

On the *dam's side* of Diomed we find three infusions of Arabian blood close up, from Godolphin Arabian, Darley's Arabian, and Alcock's Arabian. Please, dear reader, fasten this truth in your mind. Then take the *sire* of Diomed, and we find in *both* his *sire* and *dam*, Godolphin Arabian close up; and a little back Leed's Arabian, Darley Arabian, Bethel's Arabian, and Byerly Turk. Now, no great, long-extended pedigree through great mongrelizations is tacked on to Diomed, but every sire and dam was Arabian blood close up; hence when the plastic Arabian blood of Diomed was bent by man's will to trot, it was able to do so with the true game do or die qualities of the Arabian.

Had Diomed landed in New York State in place of Virginia, and his get been used to stage-coaches as were Messenger's, it is a question whether it would not have been almost the equal of Messenger. With me, as an individual, it would not, because the special pliability of Messenger blood was greater, being purer Arabian and more of the one family, Godolphin.

To-day, these blood instincts with influences, are gone. It is folly to talk of Messenger blood, or of Diomed blood influences in our trotting-horses of the present time. They are uncertainties from a multitude of mongrelizations, which no amount of printers' ink in pedigrees can purify or make more positive. Uncertainty induced our "time standard," which is like the chip on the boy's shoulder, with his bravado, "Knock it off if you dare!"

Let us simile the printed horse pedigrees of to-day by naming dogs. Horses are horses, dogs are dogs, and game-cocks are game-cocks. I have bred them all to blood, and know practically what I am writing about.

We will say that I have a remarkable pointer bitch. (I have owned and bred many.) I will take one sent to me as a little puppy many years ago by Commodore Foxhall A. Parker, of the United States Navy (deceased). His word was sufficient as to her breeding. I grew her, thoroughly house-breaking her, then presented her to Colonel J. James La Rue, of West Virginia. She was bred to blood, and proved a worker in the field from the word go. We will imagine her pedigree much as the long pedigrees of horses seem to me in catalogues and stud-books. We will say her sire was a bull-terrier out of a King Charles slut. Her grandsire was an Italian greyhound out of a black-and-tan slut. Her great-grandsire was a spitz out of an Irish setter, and so on; take them all in as one very expensive catalogue by a horse-breeder of great repute does in extended pedigrees, but best explained thus:

Saint Bernard, Newfoundland, mastiff, English bull-dog, pointer, setter, greyhound, Russian blood-hound, Scotch deer-hound, French poodle, Dutch beagle, Spanish blood-hound, Scotch terrier, water-spaniel, cocker, fox-hound, otter-hound, two cur dogs, Skye terrier, pug, colly dog, harrier, fox-terrier, English pointer, and the bitch sent to me by Commodore Parker which I presented to Colonel La Rue as a thoroughbred pointer!

Now, these names represent dogs, and many a man would accept the breeding of the pointer slut just as I here make it up, were they to read it in print. I am knowing to a great many deceptions in the breedings of horses fully as ridiculous as I here illustrate through mixing of dogs. Alfred, imported by Thomas Weddle in 1833, was an English draught-horse. In these days he figures in paper pedigrees as "Sir Alfred," the imported English thoroughbred. Turk, also imported by him at the same time, was a Cleveland Bay (as was Bellfounder, imported ten years earlier). In these days he figures as an English thoroughbred, and the get of both these horses was taken into Kentucky for stock purposes, also into the East and the West. General Dudley and Henry Clay, Jr., both took such horses from here into Kentucky, where the Alfred and Turk stock were well liked.

Imported Emigrant was another of the Alfred type; but to-day he figures as the thoroughbred English horse "Imported Emigrant."

Men are not all interested in breeding of horses or dogs; but some who have acquired wealth, gratify a latent desire for a horse or dog, then, with greater ignorance than a boy, accept printed pedigrees as authentic, contending with great energy for their truthfulness.

The mixing of all these dogs as I have given them, is but "crossing and out-crossing," as advocated by some papers. Each well-bred horse has a type of its own, which can be crossed out then back upon; but to create a new and self-sustaining type, resort must be had to the primitive. One cannot get far away from a primitive, then resort to it with *speedily* satisfactory results. It was from knowing this that I selected my mares with so great care to stint to General U. S. Grant's Arabians.

I will tell you of another move I made before, at the time, and after I had bred to General Grant's Arabians. I owned Jack Sheppard, Ashland, Black Henry, and Rushmore, each a son of Henry Clay. To these I added Baltimore's Henry Clay or Hepburn, and Spink, by Andy Johnson by Henry Clay. I had mares by Old Henry, which I stinted to these horses. I then added Clay Pilot by Neave's Clay by Cassius M. Clay by Henry Clay, to secure the Pilot blood. I had in the mean time selected choice mares by the best *sons* of Henry Clay which were *dead;* they were Harrison Clay, Madison Clay, and Colonel Wadsworth.

With the get of these sons of Henry Clay out of my better-bred mares by Henry Clay and his sons, I sold to Henry C. Jewett & Co., of Buffalo, Black Henry, Rushmore, and Ashland, also Sailor by Ashland, urging them, as the stallions were old, to breed Clay blood close, if they could get the mares. But they were strongly impressed with the cry of "cross and out-cross," as public opinion and public prejudice were financially important to them; so I ceased to speak, pursuing my own course marked out. I knew that breeding to an uncertainty, with any amount of capital at the back, must be failure in the end; and that to breed to a certainty, with no capital, could be no worse.

My close breeding of Clay was very satisfactory. The foals came in excellent form,—strong, healthy, and active, growing up handsomer, finer, and larger than the parent stock, every one showing strong trotting instinct.

I was fortunate in that my inbreeding of Clay gave me almost every time a filly, while my Arab get came horses. This attempt dates from 1880, so that my first are now past four years old, and so down to sucklings. To accomplish my purpose I had to keep all produce. My old stock represented the choicest possible selections, which I would not sell; then to part with my inbred fillies, was to rob my Arabian Clay stallion colts. and frustrate my attempts.

My purse was short; and but for the Hon. Erastus Corning, of Albany, F. P. Freeman, of New York, and L. B. Ashley, of Rochester, I should have been unable to continue to this time. It has been a long hold. The privations I have endured, the physical labor I have undergone, the large amount of public and private writing I have accomplished have been little compared with the unjust, untruthful, and cruel attacks through sporting journals; but I have stood up to it all, and now look upon my labors as having been productive of good results. I have had one good, faithful man: and what he lacked in some ways I made up, thankful he was temperate and faithful. It took courage, firmness, and concentrated purpose, with quite a little information; and at this writing I am very bold to say that no such collection in one family of horses, each and every one true to its type and pure in its blood, upon which to found and establish a national horse, has before been known upon this continent. Neither the English thoroughbred running-horse, nor the French Percheron draught-horse, nor the Russian Orloff trotting-horse were equally well founded; besides which, it is *purely American* as a foundation. It boasts of no English creation, nor French, nor Russian; but does boast of the one primitive horse, the Arabian, from which, as I have said, each one of these other nations created their "national idols;" for a good, pure-bred horse will be idolized by man.

I have concentrated my lifetime experience upon this object, that others might be benefited; and not for a purpose of financial gain to myself, as many have thought.

That the laborer is worthy of his hire I do believe; and so feeling, trust that all my labor will not have been lost.

I am getting to be an old man from continued hard work, mental and physical; and when I say that for ten years I have not had one single day of recreation, the reader can gather some idea of what my applications have been.

Some have felt hard towards me because my stallions were not for public service. Such as were old, I desired should be vigorous for my use. My Arabs I declined, because if to be condemned, I preferred it should be through the virgin mares I had grown for them, and which I believed would be impossible. I have long felt that our manner of breeding horses demanded a change; that intelligent reasons should be introduced among such breeders, as govern those interested in cattle and sheep. We have been long breeding mongrels of no fixed type of value, and ultimate results must prove financially disastrous to the agricultural country, as well as to those who are making a specialty of breeding horses of mixed bloods.

The motto, "Fewer and better," should be hung up in the office and stable of every breeder; then the occupation would grow more scientific in its tendency, with more pleasant and profitable results. No man can afford to breed and raise coach- and road-horses at seventy-five, one hundred, or one hundred and fifty dollars per head at a selling age; and yet, from our present way of breeding, it will be exceptionally good ones to bring those prices.

In closing this article I would have every breeder in the land consider me his friend. I can sympathize with them in their troubles, for I know them from practical experience. No other breeder has so many. The trials, disappointments, and vexations are greater than in any other occupation, in which they can have little sympathy from the financial, commercial, or social world. Indeed, outside their own calling they can have little intercourse, and that is not always companionable.

As I have said, I am growing old fast; and would make a suggestion, that a syndicate of younger men of means, interested in the breeding of horses, should take my entire foundation as it is to-day, then build up from it a "national horse" to their own credit, and to the credit of the country, to which the name of General U. S. Grant would be a base, and to whose memory this book is dedicated.

Having introduced a transcript from old English records relating to the foundation of their thoroughbred race-horse, I have, with permission, taken portions from General Smith's genealogical tabulation for his Golddust stallion, extending them somewhat from my own records.

By them, gentlemen who have been accustomed to cite Sir Archy, American Eclipse, Duroc, Diomed, or other thoroughbred running-horses as the blood cause for superior merit in our coach-, road-, and trotting-horse, will the more easily understand my preaching of Arabian blood *direct*.

It is also a recorded fact in English turf history, that such sires as were most closely related to their imported Arabian stallions were the getters of their highest rates of speed, with endurance. The tables I have given, showing prominent thoroughbred running-horses, are necessarily in part the foundation of our great American trotting-horse; but with me it does not seem necessary to take the blood *cause* in that way, for it is too expensive, and too far-fetched. Strike from the shoulder! Messenger, we know, was positive for trot; he was triply inbred to the Arab. Andrew Jackson and his best son, Henry Clay, were, like imported Messenger, close-bred to Arabian blood,—were born trotters, which blood instinct they gave strongly to their get from any and all classes of dams. I will, in brief, tabulate them. Again, L. L. Dorsey's old Golddust so strongly verifies my argument, I will also introduce him in genealogical tabulation, which brings in the famous Justin Morgan.

In speaking of Justin Morgan, permit me to state that from my earliest boyhood old men spoke of him as an Arabian-bred horse. I was born within five miles of where Justin Morgan was got and foaled, —*i.e.*, Springfield, Massachusetts. My father, grandfather, great- and great-great-grandfathers were all born between Springfield, Massachusetts, and Hartford, Connecticut. None were horse-dealers, but all owned and loved good horses. As a family, they were remarked for good memory and cultured intelligence. Fifty years ago, as a boy, I would listen to these old gentlemen in Springfield as they talked about the Arabian-bred "Morgan horses," and many was the one I rode or drove.

Study, observation, and practical experience with my sons and daughters of General Grant's Arabian stallions, refreshes memory, confirming my belief in the statements by these old gentlemen regarding the Arabian breeding of Justin Morgan. First, the get of Arabian stallions are small in inches, but powerful in muscular development. Their heads are fine and good, and their ears are small. From fourteen to fourteen and three-quarters is the usual height. One rising to fifteen and one-quarter or fifteen and one-half is very large for an Arab-*bred* horse. They are short in the back, are well ribbed up, and powerfully compact in build. Justin Morgan had all these points. Any one of my sons and daughters of General Grant's Arabs, would pass in Vermont for highly-bred Morgan horses, although Hegira would be considered very large. Three of them are duplicates of old-time pen-pictures of Justin Morgan.

L. L. Dorsey's old Golddust, which I have spoken of, is a happy illustration of the principle in animal life of once out and thrice back to a primitive blood. If Justin Morgan had been the product of English thoroughbred running-horse blood far removed from Arabian, why is it that the Morgan type could never in any way be duplicated in England or America by or through crosses from the English thoroughbred fixed type? Still, the Morgan horse retains his characteristics widely different from any thoroughbred race-horse crosses.

Besides Messenger, Morgan, and Dorsey's old Golddust, each a representative of close-bred Arabian product, we have Andrew Jackson and his best son, Henry Clay. Now, every horseman knows that each one of these five different Arab-bred stallions were natural trotters, and to the end of time produced instinctive trot in their get; with all, the first get by each representative Arab-bred horse were famous quarter horses at the running gait. Is there no reason in our arguments?

Were it not for vexing my publishers through annoyance to their compositors and proof-readers, I would introduce a number of genealogical tabulations, but I have already burdened them beyond an apology.

It is a lamentable fact that serious errors will creep into print, which lead many breeders to great disappointment; but such errors are unavoidable. In speaking of the Morgan horse (although I have overstepped my contract with my publishers as to number of pages), I will tell of one serious error and explain it. Thomas H. Kellogg was born in Sheffield, Massachusetts, in 1773, moving to East Bloomfield, Ontario County, about 1800. He was a large farmer and great horseman; always keeping one or two stallions for public service. These he would bring from the East (Long Island and New England was then called the East). In 1826 he brought from Boston a son of Justin Morgan that had been raised in Vermont. Mr. Kellogg stood this horse as "Kellogg's son of Justin Morgan," or as the "Morgan horse." In 1828 the Morgan abduction (Masonic) involved his son-in-law, Colonel Edward Sawyer, of Canandaigua (eight miles distant). Prejudice ran very high against the name of Morgan, so that even the name of Mr. Kellogg's stallion was a damage to him; then too, Colonel Sawyer being a son-in-law of Thomas H. Kellogg, his Morgan stallion was in danger. It was advised to change the name; and as this country was full of Scotchmen, the name of "*Highlander*" was given to Kellogg's son of Justin Morgan. It was a big move, and as anything brought from the East into this then far West was said to be *imported*, they soon spoke of Thomas Kellogg's horse as the "imported horse Highlander." By him were got Shelton's Highlander, Paul's Highlander, Baker's Highlander, with innumerable sons and daughters, and grandsons and granddaughters, to be scattered East and West as by "imported Highlander," and later as by "thoroughbred Highlander;" even the old horse himself went West as "imported Highlander." This is the thoroughbred Highlander blood in the grandam of George Wilkes. These truths I am knowing to, as are plenty of other old men. T. H. Kellogg died in East Bloomfield in 1857, eighty-four years old, and his daughter Mary long resided with my father-in-law.

In these days I never see the name of "Highlander" in the breeding of any trotting-horse East or West, without wondering to myself whether the blood came from Uncle Thomas Kellogg's son of the Arabian-bred Justin Morgan. There are so many errors in the recorded breedings of noted horses that I am knowing to, as in the above instance, that I am a very sceptical man in matters of recorded pedigrees. One of the greatest brood mares in America, as a producer of the highest rates of trotting speed in every colt, by any horse, is recorded with a long pedigree which I know to be positively false; for both herself and dam were bred and raised near me, and I know all about them; but because thoroughbred running-horse blood is so fashionable in the sire or dam, her pedigree is loaded with it, in print. Her owner is one of the prominent men in the country, and to attack the pedigree of his wonderful brood mare would injure me, without doing any good. In another instance, where I wrote the owner that the breeding of his horse as advertised to the public was a mistake, showing him where, he replied by letter, which I still have, saying, "My horse has a good pedigree and is recorded. Until a man can give me a better one, his advertised breeding will not be changed." Now, no man need fear me, for I prefer to die with these errors unrevealed rather than endure any more injustice than I have, from trying to help breeders at large, through telling them where their "Chester white" was a "Berkshire bred" to my personal knowledge.

"Blood Will Tell."

"CLAYRABIA," AND "CLAYBEALE GRANT." 59

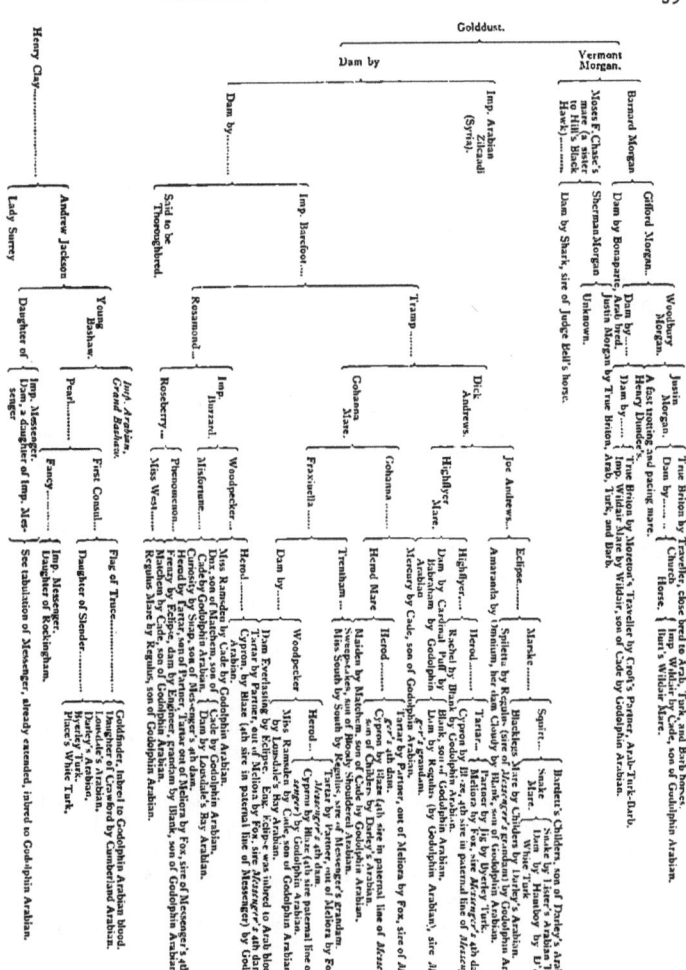

OLD "HENRY CLAY."

The likeness of the stallion Henry Clay, known as Colonel William W. Wadsworth's Henry Clay for many years, but of late as Old Henry Clay, is the only correct picture of the horse presented to the public eye. Henry Clay was Arabian-bred, strongly so; possessing the build, disposition, and constitution of the Arab. His ears were fine and small, forehead full and broad, jowls deep, wide between, and thin; eyes large and prominent, muzzle small, with thin lips, and large thin nostrils. His limbs were fine, yet powerful; the osselets small, as in the Arabian; while his very handsome feet were tough enough to go for all time barefoot, a peculiarity of the Arab. He was the founder of the entire family of Clay horses, and his purity of blood was so great as to stamp his high physical qualities with instincts to a positiveness, outlasting that of all other families to date.

In 1846 and 1847, Mr. T. K. Van Zant, of Albany, New York, then a rising young artist, was employed by Miss Wadsworth (sister of William W. Wadsworth) to paint some blooded cattle and sheep, for her. At this time, Mr. Wadsworth requested that Henry Clay should be painted as he stood *in his stall.* The painting was large and attractive. Sitting in front of the horse was a white terrier dog, a companion of Henry, and pet with Mr. Wadsworth. Upon the harness-pegs in the stall was a bridle; and in the door-way were brushes and comb, and an open window gave a charming perspective view, so that as a whole, the painting pleased Mr. Wadsworth, although the horse as represented, was but a poor attempt by an amateur. Such was the Wadsworth painting. However, when we consider Mr. Van Zant's limited experience at that time, also his physical infirmities (neither fingers nor thumb), we must say that he deserves both credit and commendation for his prominence as an animal painter in later years. My introduction of Henry Clay into this book may be considered out of place; but when it is understood that the horse was strongly inbred to Arabian blood in both sires and dams, and was but a third remove from an imported

thoroughbred Arabian, and that, through the dams, Henry Clay was superior in blood to imported Messenger, and as an individual horse was of far greater merit, I am certain the reader will approve the subject as happily introduced.

As my long-looked for "Clay History," with between seventy and eighty sketches of sons and daughters and grandsons and granddaughters (by the lamented Herbert S. Kittredge), will at some time appear, it would be out of place were I to make this souvenir to General U. S. Grant, a place for controversy as to the merit or demerit of the Clay family of horses.

The Arabians Leopard and Linden, were sketched in 1880, as illustrative of Arabian blood influence, for my contemplated "Clay History;" and for that purpose the drawings were then secured by copyright, little dreaming they would become objects of special interest to the public through the untimely taking away of the people's idol, General U. S. Grant.

As Herbert S. Kittredge progressed with his sketches for my "Clay History," he was mostly among old men who knew Henry Clay and had bred to him. In *their* telling him of the horse, and often pointing out striking resemblance in some son or daughter, Kittredge grew to know Henry Clay without having seen him.

Now, the mind of Kittredge was peculiar. He rarely would talk, but would absorb the mind and thoughts of such as talked interestingly to him. I often felt that the object in the minds of others was so photographed upon his own, that with his pencil he could reproduce the subject *à la Nast*. Numerous instances of this gift occurred during his three years' residence with me, which I noted down. He was what might be termed a mind-reader in art. One case of many, where he was put to a test. I will cite as interesting.

Early in December, 1880, Mr. Orrin Hickok sent me from San Francisco, California, a very large lithograph of Saint Julian. It was badly out of proportion, not looking like the horse. I hung it in Kittredge's studio in my house, pointing out to him where it was wrong, and how he could make a good likeness of Saint Julian from it. When he went to New York City that winter, I told him to take the picture, hang it in his room, and get Mr. Goldsmith to come and criticise it. I met Mr. Goldsmith there, and through our criticism a perfect sketch was made for me, which to-day is unequalled as a likeness of the horse.

During the next season, when Saint Julian was in the circuit and had reached Buffalo, Kittredge went from my residence to that city and sketched the horse from life. When Mr. Hickok and Saint Julian reached Rochester, we met Mr. Goldsmith, Mr. Hickok, and others in Saint Julian's box, with the two sketches,—one made through criticism upon the lithograph, and the other from life. The *conception* sketch was the most perfect. Both being the same size, none could tell which was the one from life; but Mr. Hickok and Mr. Goldsmith pronounced my sketch as most perfect of the horse, and later, many duplicates were made by Kittredge from my sketch, by tracing through oiled paper, after the manner adopted for *pirating* sketches, pictures, and paintings.

I had borrowed from Mr. W. A. Wadsworth, in 1879, his father's old painting of Henry Clay, in order that H. S. Kittredge might sketch a copy to serve as frontispiece to my "Clay History;" and at once secured it by copyright for that purpose, to which Mr. Wadsworth had donated it. This painting I hung in my dining-room, so Kittredge would see it every time he sat at my table. To forward my ends, I. invited Mr. Worthington, Mr. Nelson Thompson, Mr. M. L. Commins, Mr. Robert Whaley, and Mr. Frederick Fellows to meet at my house and criticise this painting for Kittredge. Four of the different gentlemen had owned Henry Clay after Mr. William W. Wadsworth's death, and all had known the horse since his arrival from Long Island at Geneseo. Mr. Ambrose Worthington kept a hotel at Geneseo, and was also a stage-route owner, mail contractor, and for fifty years the best coach-horse matcher in Western New York. Such a man is a good critic. Mr. Nelson Thompson, of Penn Yan, was his partner at one time in the stage business. Mr. Thompson, after Mr. Wadsworth's death, wanted Henry Clay, and through Mr. Worthington, who lived at Geneseo, he got him, only half an hour before John Purchase of Long Island walked into the office with money in hand, intending to take the stallion back to Long Island, where he had been taking his colts by the dozen as yearlings, every year since Henry Clay came into this country. Whatever became of all of Henry Clay's colts that John Purchase took to Long Island between 1846 and the time of Colonel Wadsworth's death, nobody knows; for John Purchase is also dead.

However, these different owners of Henry Clay came repeatedly to see me and to tell Kittredge over and over again, where Van Zant's painting failed of being correct.

Kittredge grew enthusiastic to make the sketch, so I removed the painting to his room. The sketch he made and brought to me was in pencil, shaded up to a finish. I was astonished at its perfectness, but had faith from the first to believe he would do it. The star was a crescent, as if to brand his princely Oriental blood. This Mr. Van Zant thought unnatural, so in his painting made it as he thought it should be, which improvements are faults with most animal painters.

With Kittredge, if there was a spavin, or curb, or capped hock, cocked ankles, goitre, blind eye, or any physical imperfection, or mark in the hoof, or in fact any identifying mark, it was certain to be in his sketch. Then, too, the length of the ear, or kink or wave in the mane and tail, appeared in the drawing as it was in the horse.

This pencil sketch was submitted to each one of these five named gentlemen, and warmly endorsed by them, as perfect. I then had Kittredge shade it up in India ink, placing it with my collection of Clay sketches, now appearing for the first time before the public, in this souvenir.

A feeling of injustice to poor "Kirby" Van Zant began to come over me. But for "Kirby" Van Zant there would have been no painting of Henry Clay from which to make this sketch. Could I not in some way befriend the old artist, even to giving him credit for this sketch in my book?

The late Daniel S. Lathrop, of Albany, was a friend of Mr. T. K. Van Zant; he was also a friend of mine, and a warm admirer of young Kittredge. I wrote Mr. Lathrop of what I had done, also of my feelings towards Van Zant, asking if it were not possible for him to make a new painting, correcting his errors so that it could appear in my work to his credit as the artist.

Mr. Lathrop replied "that Van Zant could not remember the horse, but thought he could correct his errors in the painting, of which he was certain there must be many, for it was a work of his youth; although, much as he would like to try, he had a dread of seeing the old painting."

Mr. Lathrop advised to send it to him, which I did. In due time he wrote requesting me to come down to Albany, as Mr. Van Zant had corrected his malformations in the old painting, in a copy; but had no recollection of the horse. I went, and soon saw that Mr. Van Zant was justly credited as a superior artist in the manipulation of colors in oil, as a landscape-painter; but was not excellent in horse portraiture, nor vivid in memory; but that some justice might be awarded to him in the matter of his old painting, I remained with him part of the day, leading a horse up to his door that he might study the position of the limbs in repose, after which I ordered him to paint me two copies, as well as he could, from Wadsworth's old painting. Mr. Lathrop, knowing I had secured the painting by copyright, asked that he might have two copies.

Both these orders were given to help Mr. Van Zant, who was needy. When the paintings for me came to hand, they were far from satisfactory to these old gentlemen critics; nothing but Kittredge's sketch would do for them, or for myself, as I remembered Old Henry, so I presented one of the two paintings to a gentleman, retaining the other. In these two *copies* Mr. Van Zant's love for scenery was such, that he would not reproduce the horse in his stable as in the original ; but made an entirely new painting, losing all semblance to the original. Kittredge, in his copy of the painting, reproduced fact (the horse in his stall). As a scenic-painter, Van Zant would be grand. Kittredge, on the other hand, would concentrate all his mind upon the one object. This I encouraged, so that most of my sketches represent the object standing upon a plain floor. I have often noticed that our very best portrait-, as well as animal-painters, failed in all but *the object;* Kittredge himself knowing this, depended upon his young associate, Andrew J. Schultz, to fill in the background where one was desired, in which Schultz excelled. The two were differently gifted; Schultz studying under Kittredge progressed rapidly in horse portraiture.

I have already said more than I intended about the sketch of Henry Clay, in this book. No horse, to my knowledge, had such a remarkable life as Henry Clay, as will appear in my history devoted to him, and for which he was sketched as a frontispiece, to be followed by over seventy representative sons, daughters, grandsons, and granddaughters, all by the master-workman, Herbert S. Kittredge.

All horsemen and readers of equine literature know what value I put upon Henry Clay; they also know that my persevering and vigorous championship has resurrected him from the oblivion to which he was rapidly being consigned, and has given him a name and fame among the different families.

Although his superior value was patent to me from the time my attention was first directly called to him as a remarkable horse and sire, I must confess that it was not until after months and even years of persistent investigation, that I discovered I must look to Arabian blood for the qualities which made Henry Clay of such unusual merit. At first I was satisfied to call it "Henry Clay," and on that name to build my foundation; but when the inquisitive and ever-insatiable public continued to ask the reason *why* I placed Henry Clay at the front, I was forced, *nolens volens*, to seek for the primitive cause, and that I have proven, to my own satisfaction at least, was due to the Arabian ancestry. So, as Henry Clay has seemed from some unaccountable reason a difficult name for the dear public to swallow (a "rose by any other name will smell as sweet"), we will call it Arab, for it must eventually merge into that. Arab or Clay, it is all the same to me so long as the blood still continues to sustain the high character I have given the horse for the future. For this reason it seems amply fitting that Henry Clay should have a place among these royal pages.

His Arabian paternity is authenticated; and upon it he has never thrown a stain; but the rather, has shone with a brilliancy fairly eclipsing those of more primitive and noble birth.

Horse lovers and breeders generally know full as well as I can tell them, how severely I have been criticised, and how bitterly I have been assailed for my strong and perhaps more ardent defence of Henry Clay than was necessary. I have never written to wound, but from the earnestness of my convictions, knowing the horse as I did, and as my opponents did not. If at any time my pen has written more harshly than it should, I crave the pardon of whoever may have been stung by its point. All I ask in return, is that those who have maligned me most, shall make the same diligent study and research that I have, and wherever they find I have spoken truthfully, will have the candor to acknowledge it; and in the course of *horse events*, should calamity overtake the valuable representatives of the blood for which I have been contending, I have still one further request to make even of my bitterest enemy: that if one or more of them shall ever fall into his hands, he will have the honesty and fairness to carry out in breeding, the principles which I have sought and proven; then, from his own actual experience say whether these things are so.

I cannot close these few pages without a word for the noble and gifted young artist whose name graces the pictures of General Grant's two Arabian stallions in this book, Herbert S. Kittredge. But for him General Grant's Arabs, Old Henry Clay, and many others would never have been reproduced in such faultless manner, so perfectly true to life. That young Kittredge is dead is a public calamity, and we feel that "we shall ne'er see his like again," although his young associate, Andrew J. Schultz, has done splendidly in an effort to fill the vacancy.

Perhaps the author of this book may be pardoned in assuming to himself the credit, not of making the artist, but of bringing him before the public, especially in horse portraiture; of encouraging his continuance to a perfecting himself in this particular direction, recognizing as we did, his remarkable gift in giving to the horse a *personnel*—if I may be allowed the expression—that we have never seen equalled by any other American artist.

I would also here thank the several journals who, during my single-handed contest for blood and breeding in our American horse, have extended to me numerous courtesies through their columns when so many of their more valuable patrons were opposed to me.

Again allow me to express to the Messrs. Lippincott my hearty satisfaction for the elegant and faithful manner in which they have represented my thoughts in the getting up of this souvenir.

                Respectfully,
                      RANDOLPH HUNTINGTON.

www.ingramcontent.com/pod-product-compliance
Lightning Source LLC
Chambersburg PA
CBHW022146090426
42742CB00010B/1415